MAR 3 1 2012

DOUGLASS-TRUTH LIBRARY

NO LONGER PROPERTY OF
SEATTLE PUBLIC LIBRARY

D0602366

Colombia

Colombia

by Marion Morrison

Enchantment of the World
Second Series

Children's Press®

A Division of Scholastic Inc.

New York   Toronto   London   Auckland   Sydney
Mexico City   New Delhi   Hong Kong
Danbury, Connecticut

Frontispiece: View from the Convent of San Agustín, Mompós, Colombia

Consultant: Herbert Braun, Department of History, University of Virginia, Charlottesville, Virginia

Please note: All statistics are as up-to-date as possible at the time of publication.

Book production by Herman Adler

Library of Congress Cataloging-in-Publication Data

Morrison, Marion.
 Colombia / by Marion Morrison.
    p. cm.—(Enchantment of the world. Second series)
 Includes bibliographical references and index.
 ISBN-13: 978-0-516-25947-5
 ISBN-10: 0-516-25947-4
 1. Colombia—Juvenile literature. I. Title. II. Series.
 F2258.5.M67 2007
 986.1—dc22   2007002300

No part of this publication may be reproduced in whole or in part, or stored in a retrieval system, or transmitted in any form or by any means, electronic, mechanical, photocopying, recording, or otherwise, without written permission of the publisher. For information regarding permission, write to Scholastic Inc., 557 Broadway, New York, NY 10012.

© 2008 by Marion Morrison.
All rights reserved. Published in 2008 by Children's Press, an imprint of Scholastic Inc.
Published simultaneously in Canada.
Printed in the United States of America. 44

SCHOLASTIC, CHILDREN'S PRESS, and associated logos are trademarks and/or registered trademarks of Scholastic Inc.

1 2 3 4 5 6 7 8 9 10 R 17 16 15 14 13 12 11 10 09 08   08

Colombia

Contents

Cover photo:
Cartagena

A house on stilts

Guambiano mother and child

Welcome to Colombia

IN 1972, A GROUP OF TREASURE HUNTERS WAS TRUDGING up the steep slopes of the Sierra Nevada de Santa Marta in northeastern Colombia. As they made their way through the thick forest, they came across long stone stairways grown over by the tangled greenery. Climbing higher, they found terraces and tombs. Inside the tombs—perhaps to their disappointment—they found not gold, but a few ancient stone necklaces. They sold the necklaces, and news of Ciudad Perdida, "Lost City," was out. The ancient city dates back to A.D. 500.

Opposite: **A guard tower from a seventeenth-century Spanish fort looms over modern Cartagena.**

To reach Ciudad Perdida, visitors climb more than 1,200 stone steps through the thick forest.

The discovery did not surprise everyone. The Sierra Nevada de Santa Marta has long been home to indigenous, or native, peoples. Three groups from this area—the Arhuaco, the Kogi, and the Arsario—survive to this day. They claim to have regularly visited Ciudad Perdida, which they call Teyuna, before its 1972 discovery. They believe it was the main city of their ancestors, the Tairona. In its prime, Ciudad Perdida may have been home to between two thousand and eight thousand people. Most likely, it was abandoned when the Spanish took over the region in the sixteenth century.

After the treasure hunters stumbled across the ancient site, workers began unearthing it. They discovered a complex system of buildings, including about 150 stone terraces that were once the foundations of houses, paved paths, and stone stairways.

Thousands of Arhuaco live on the slopes of the Sierra Nevada de Santa Marta. They are among the most traditional of Colombia's native peoples.

Ciudad Perdida quickly became a popular tourist attraction. Some of the local native groups, who are not always welcoming to outsiders, seemed happy enough to meet the visitors.

All was well until something happened that highlighted the problems

One of the strongest rebel groups in Colombia is the Army of National Liberation, known as the ELN. The group has been active since the 1960s.

that have beset Colombia for decades. In September 2003, one of Colombia's rebel groups kidnapped eight foreign tourists who were trekking to Ciudad Perdida.

Rebel groups have been operating in Colombia for decades. These left-wing groups want to overthrow the government and establish a communist state, one in which the government owns most businesses and controls the economy. Opposing them are violent right-wing groups. As a result, the country has been in an ongoing state of civil war. Tens of thousands of people have been killed. More than three million people have been pushed off their land or have fled the fighting. Colombia has the highest kidnapping and murder rates in the world.

Colombia's troubles don't stop there. The country is also the center of the world's cocaine trade. Cocaine, an illegal drug, is derived from coca, a leafy plant that grows mainly in the valleys and slopes of the Andes Mountains in Bolivia and Peru. For centuries, native Andean peoples have chewed dried coca leaves mixed with lime or ash to stave off hunger and cold. Chewing coca leaves also plays an important part in their religious ceremonies. Some modern-day travelers drink coca tea to help ward off altitude sickness, an illness people sometimes get at high elevations.

Some coca is grown in Colombia. More often, coca is grown in Peru and Bolivia and then sent to Colombia to be processed into cocaine in factories hidden in the forests. The cocaine is shipped to the United States, Europe, and elsewhere around the world.

Colombia's drug trafficking has been controlled for many years by gangs in Cali and Medellín, two of the country's largest cities. Huge amounts of money change hands, and the rivalry between the drug-running groups has caused great upheaval in the country. No one who tries to bring the criminals to justice is safe. Even judges fear for their lives. Some drug runners have been caught, but despite support from the U.S. Drug Enforcement Agency (DEA) and advice from experts worldwide, the drug trade continues.

Workers uproot and destroy coca plants in the Cauca Mountains southwest of Bogotá. Their work is part of the effort to control the illegal drug trade.

COLOMBIA

- ● Cities of over 500,000 people
- ○ Other cities
- ✪ National capital

0   200 miles

0   200 kilometers

Caribbean Sea

NETHERLANDS
ANTILLES

Tayrona
National
Park

Ríohacha

Santa Marta

Barranquilla

Sierra Nevada de Santa Marta
National Park

Sabanalarga

Cartagena

Arjona

Valledupar

Carmen

Lorica

Sincelejo

Catatumbo Barí
National Park

Montería

El Banco

VENEZUELA

Turbo

Ocaña

N

Caucasia

Cúcuta

*Paramillo
National Park*

Pamplona

Tama National Park

Barrancabermeja

W   E

Bucaramanga

Arauca

S

Medellín

Cocuy National Park

*PACIFIC
OCEAN*

Nuquí

Quibdó

Sonsón

Tunja

Sogamoso

Puerto
Carreño

Manizales

Zipaquirá

Yopal

El Tuparro
National Park

Pereira

Armero

Bogotá

Armenia

Ibagué

Villavicencio

Buenaventura

Buga

Palmira

*Farallones de Cali
National Park*

Cali

*Sumapaz
National Park*

Puerto
Inírida

Tierradentro

Neiva

*Sierra de la
Macarena
National Park*

Guaviare R.

Popayán

*Cordillera de los Picachos
National Park*

San José del Guaviare

Tumaco

*Puracé
National Park*

Garzón

*Tinigua
National Park*

Calamar

San
Felipe

San Agustín

Florencia

*Serranía de
Chiribiquete
National Park*

Mitú

Pasto

Mocoa

Ipiales

ECUADOR

*La Pnya
National Park*

La Tagua

Araracuara

BRAZIL

Caquetá R.

*Cahuinari
National
Park*

La Pedrera

El Encanto

*Río Puré
National
Park*

Putumayo R.

Amazon R.

PERU

*Amacayacu
National Park*

Leticia

Magdalena R.

Orinoco R.

Colombia

President Álvaro Uribe Vélez won reelection in 2006 with 62 percent of the vote. His father, a wealthy rancher, was killed by rebels in 1983.

Since the 1980s, rival groups have grown marijuana—also an illegal drug—and coca on the lower slopes of the Sierra Nevada de Santa Marta. The mountains have become a battleground for the warring groups. The local indigenous peoples have frequently been caught in the crossfire. One Arsario village was destroyed.

Over the years, Colombia's leaders have worked to resolve the problems of the rebel groups and the drug traffickers. President Álvaro Uribe Vélez, who was elected in 2002 and again in 2006, has been the most successful. He has taken a hard line against the fighters, no matter what their politics are. This has proved successful. Colombia has seen a sharp drop in kidnappings and murders in recent years.

Tourists are once again trekking to Ciudad Perdida. The number of foreign visitors to Colombia jumped 65 percent between 2002 and 2005. In 2006, one million international visitors arrived in the country. This interest in Colombia results partly from a new tourism campaign that highlights Colombia's many attractions. These include the intriguing colonial city of Cartagena de Indias on the Caribbean coast and the treasure trove of ancient gold artifacts found in the Gold Museum in Bogotá, Colombia's capital.

Colombia has as many scenic wonders as any country in South America. The towering Andes Mountains cut across the country. Rain forests in the Amazon region in the south and the Chocó region in the west are home to an astonishing variety of wildlife.

About 1,800 bird species have been spotted in Colombia, more than in any other country in the world. Unfortunately, much of the birds' habitat is also suitable for growing coca. The Colombian government is trying to ensure that the birds survive, and that the drug trade does not.

A golden replica of a ceremonial raft used long ago by the native Muisca people is one of the highlights of the Gold Museum.

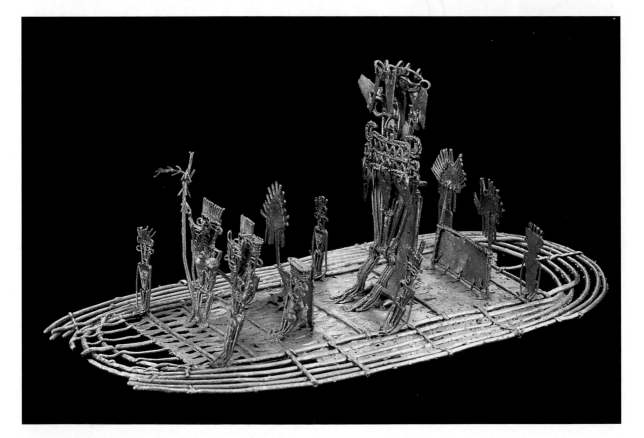

Country of Contrasts

Steep cliffs rise from the waters of the Caribbean near Santa Marta, in north-western Colombia.

THE REPUBLIC OF COLOMBIA IS NAMED AFTER THE explorer Christopher Columbus. His name in Spanish is Cristóbal Colón. Colombia lies in the north of South America. It is the continent's fourth-largest country.

Colombia shares borders with Venezuela and Brazil to the east and Ecuador and Peru to the south. In the northwest, in a wild region known as the Darién, Colombia connects to Panama. The Isthmus of Panama is the narrow neck of land that links Central and South America. Colombia also borders the Pacific Ocean in the west and the Caribbean Sea in the north.

Opposite: **Providencia, a mountainous island in the Caribbean Sea, is a popular vacation spot.**

Colombia's Geographic Features

Area: 439,735 square miles (1,138,908 sq km)

Largest City: Bogotá, 6,778,691

Highest Elevation: Pico Cristóbal Colón, 19,020 feet (5,797 m) above sea level

Lowest Elevation: Sea level, along the coasts

Longest Navigable River: Magdalena River, 956 miles (1,538 km) long, navigable for more than 930 miles (1,497 km)

Highest Waterfall: Candelas Falls, 984 feet (300 m), on the Cusiana River

Lowest Average Temperature: 46°F (8°C) in January, in Bogotá

Highest Average Temperature: 92°F (33°C) in July, in Cali

Highest Average Annual Rainfall: Chocó, 324 inches (823 cm)

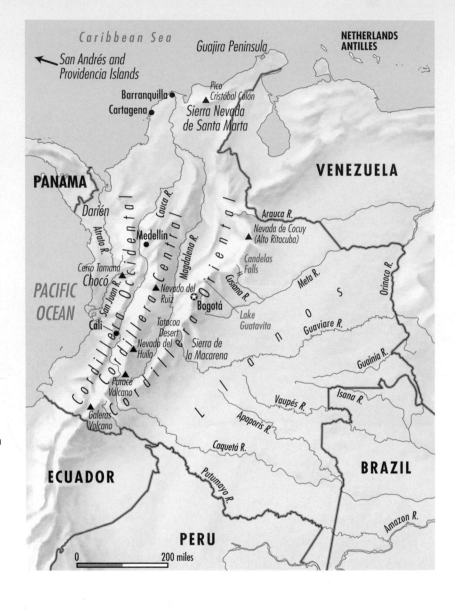

The Andes

The Andes Mountains stretch 4,500 miles (7,200 kilometers) across the length of South America, reaching all the way from Venezuela in the north to the southernmost tip of the continent. The Andes stretch down the entire west coast of Colombia.

In Colombia, the Andes split into three *cordilleras* ("mountain ranges"). The farthest east and the largest is the Cordillera Oriental. Next to it is the Cordillera Central. And in the west is the Cordillera Occidental, the lowest of the three ranges.

The Cordillera Oriental

The Cordillera Oriental curves to the southwest as it cuts across Colombia all the way from Venezuela to Ecuador. The highest peak in the Cordillera Oriental is Alto Ritacuba, at 18,021 feet (5,493 meters). It rises amid a cluster of snowy summits in the Sierra Nevada de Cocuy, near the Venezuelan border. On a high plateau in the middle of the Cordillera Oriental stands the capital city of Bogotá, 8,563 feet (2,610 m) above sea level.

With a population of nearly seven million, Bogotá is by far the largest city in Colombia. It is more than three times larger than Medellín, the next largest city.

Low ranges surround Bogotá. To the east, their slopes descend abruptly through forests to vast, low-lying prairies called *Llanos*. Rivers flow from the mountains across the Llanos to the Orinoco River, which forms part of the Colombia-Venezuela border. To the south, other rivers flow eastward toward the Amazon basin.

The Cordillera Central

The Cordillera Central has many volcanoes. The highest, the Nevado del Huila, soars to 18,865 feet (5,750 m). Puracé Volcano, which rises to 15,604 feet (4,756 m), towers over the historic town of Popayán.

In 1983, Popayán was struck by an earthquake that caused hundreds of deaths. Most recently, Colombia's deadliest natural disaster occurred when the Nevado del Ruiz Volcano erupted in 1985, killing twenty-five thousand people.

Popayán is known as the "White City" because of its many beautiful white buildings from the colonial era.

The Armero Disaster

Armero was once a quiet town on the slopes of the Nevado del Ruiz Volcano. People there grew coffee, potatoes, and cotton. In November 1985, the volcano erupted, melting about 10 percent of its icy cap. The melting ice cap resulted in a mudflow that sent millions of tons of melted ice, slush, and volcanic debris on a deadly high-speed run downhill. The mud formed a wave 15 feet (4.6 m) high. This mud wave swept over Armero and a nearby village, burying people in their homes as they slept. Twenty-five thousand people died in Armero. The town has never been rebuilt. Dozens of crosses now dot the eerie landscape.

The Cordillera Occidental

The Cordillera Occidental runs parallel to the Pacific Ocean, from Panama to Ecuador. Its highest point is Cerro Tamana, at 13,780 feet (4,200 m). A narrow strip of low land separates its foothills from the sea.

The Galeras Volcano, one of the most active volcanoes in Colombia, is in the south of this range, close to the small city of Pasto. In 1993, the volcano erupted, killing nine people and severely damaging nearby crops and homes.

Antonio Nariño

The city of Pasto is the capital of Nariño Department in Colombia's southern highlands. *Department* is Colombia's word for "state" or "province." Nariño Department is named after Antonio Nariño, a leader in Colombia's fight for independence from Spain.

Antonio Nariño was born in Bogotá in 1765. Before he was thirty, he had translated Thomas Paine's pamphlet *The Rights of Man*, which argued against monarchies and in favor of democratic governments. The Spanish authorities caught him distributing it and threw him in prison in Spain. He escaped and went into hiding in England and France. He returned to Colombia as the independence movement gathered pace, only to be placed under house arrest. He was finally released in 1810 and immediately opened a political newspaper.

Later, he became a commander of the forces fighting for independence. He almost lost his life in a battle near Pasto in 1814. Once again, he was

captured and thrown into prison, where he languished until 1820. By that time the country had won its independence. Nariño died in 1823. He was one of Colombia's best-loved leaders.

The Sierra Nevada de Santa Marta

The Sierra Nevada de Santa Marta rises in northern Colombia. The first European explorers to arrive in the region saw the mountain range's snowy peaks from many miles out at sea. Colombia's highest mountain, Pico Cristóbal Colón, is in the Sierra Nevada de Santa Marta. It is 19,020 feet (5,797 m) high.

The range's western side has many small rivers that rush down to the lowlands. This is a land of shallow lagoons and large swamps.

The northern Sierra Nevada de Santa Marta is a scrub-covered peninsula called the Guajira. Colombia and Venezuela split this desert region, which juts into the Caribbean. It is Colombia's only large desert area.

The Llanos

The Llanos are exceptionally flat prairies that spread out across eastern Colombia. They extend into Venezuela, creating the largest grassland in South America.

The Llanos lie east of the Andes. Together with the Amazon region, they make up about two-thirds of Colombia.

Villavicencio, at the foot of the Cordillera Oriental, is considered the capital of the Llanos region. It is only 69 miles (111 km) from Bogotá, and a spectacular mountain road connects the two cities. The paved highway continues a few miles beyond Villavicencio, and then nothing but grasslands stretches to the horizon. Though unpaved tracks cut across the grasslands, many are impassable in the wet season.

Colombia's Amazon

The mighty Amazon River flows across the northern part of South America. It is the second-longest river in the world, and by far the largest in terms of the amount of water it carries and the area it drains. The Amazon makes up only about 50 miles (80 km) of Colombia's border, but dozens of rivers that flow into the Amazon begin in Colombia's mountains. One of these, the Putumayo River, begins on the eastern slopes of the Andes and tumbles down through dense forests to the lowlands, where it forms part of Colombia's border with Ecuador and Peru.

The Amazon River floods frequently. Some Colombians build their houses on stilts to protect them from floodwaters.

The Rubber Boom

One of the Amazon region's most valuable products is rubber. Rubber is made from latex sap that is drained from rubber trees.

During the 1800s, rubber became a valuable product. The process of vulcanization, which gives rubber its strength and flexibility, made it especially suitable for the rainproof clothes and boots fashionable at the time. When the bicycle and then the car were invented, a huge demand arose for rubber tires. The rubber boom was on.

The best rubber came from the Amazon forests, where business owners forced indigenous peoples to collect rubber sap. These rubber barons amassed great fortunes.

For years, Colombia and Peru argued over an area around the Putumayo River where some of the best rubber trees were located. Eventually, it was decided that Leticia, Colombia's city in the Amazon region, would stay part of Colombia.

The principal Colombian town in the Amazon region is Leticia. It is accessible to the rest of the country only by plane or by an uncomfortable boat and bus journey.

The Chocó

The Chocó region lies between the Pacific Ocean and the Cordillera Occidental. It stretches from the swamps of the Darién southward for about 550 miles (900 km). The land is mostly flat, though some hills rise in the southern Chocó. The coastline is fringed with swamps, lagoons, and other wetlands.

Chocó forests are a tangle of greenery.

Countless species of animals and plants abound in the Chocó region's dense rain forests. Many of the plants are world-record holders. One plant has leaves that are more than 3 feet (1 m) long and 20 inches (50 centi-meters) wide!

An average of 324 inches (823 cm) of rain falls in the Chocó every year. In the record year of 1939, 593 inches (1,506 cm) fell. The Chocó is probably the largest wet region on Earth. The heavy rain drains into spectacular rivers that crash through canyons in a series of waterfalls and rapids.

These rivers carry enormous quantities of water. The San Juan and Atrato rivers, which almost meet near the city of Quibdó, were once used as a route between the Caribbean and the Pacific. A person could travel south on the Atrato from the Caribbean and then move overland to the San Juan and travel its course to the Pacific.

Looking at Colombia's Cities

Medellín (below right) is Colombia's second-largest city, with a population of 2,223,660. It was founded in 1616 by Spanish settlers. Today, it is the center of Colombia's textile industry. It is also a center for coffee and food processing. Medellín has many museums, including the Museum of Modern Art and the Museum of Anthropology. It is sometimes called the City of Eternal Spring because it enjoys an average year-round temperature of 71 degrees Fahrenheit (22 degrees Celsius).

Cali (above), which is home to 2,075,380 people, is Colombia's third-largest city. It was founded in 1536 by explorer Sebastián de Belalcázar. Today, the city is a center of industry, farming, and trade in the southwest of the country. It is famous for salsa music, and Cali residents take pride in their city's bullfighting ring, the largest in the country.

Barranquilla, which was founded in 1629, is Colombia's main Caribbean seaport and a center of the textile industry. The nation's fourth-largest city, it has a population of 1,113,016. Hot, wet weather with an average year-round temperature of 82°F (28°C) often makes life uncomfortable in Barranquilla.

The Magdalena River, the largest river in Colombia, rises in the far south of the Cordillera Central. The river then flows north for 956 miles (1,538 km) before entering the Caribbean near the port of Barranquilla. On its lower course, the Magdalena is wide and shallow. By the time the river empties into the sea, it has divided into one main channel and a maze of smaller waterways and lagoons.

The Cauca River also starts in the southern Cordillera Central. It flows 838 miles (1,348 km) northward through rich land before joining the Magdalena in flatlands about 120 miles (193 km) from the sea.

The Magdalena River flows into the Caribbean Sea at Barranquilla. The river's mouth is dredged to ensure that oceangoing ships can make their way up the river.

The Islands

Several islands belong to Colombia. The largest are San Andrés and Providencia, which lie in the Caribbean Sea about 480 miles (770 km) northwest of Barranquilla. The islands are actually closer to Nicaragua in Central America, and the two nations have long disputed who owns them.

Other small islands are nearer the Colombian mainland. The most visited are the Islas del Rosario, which are near the historic city of Cartagena on the Caribbean coast.

The Pacific coast has a few small islands, most of them near the shore. The most famous is Gorgona Island, which was once used as a prison but is now a national park. Gorgona is a scuba divers' paradise. Another island, Malpelo, is less than 1 mile (1.6 km) long and lies 300 miles (480 km) off the port of Buenaventura.

A bridge connects Providencia Island with the smaller Santa Catalina Island. People visit the islands to enjoy swimming, diving, and simply relaxing.

A Wealth of Wildlife

COLOMBIA HAS A WEALTH OF WILDLIFE THAT IS unrivaled around the globe. The country covers only 1 percent of Earth's surface, but holds 15 percent of the world's known species. Thirty-three percent of Colombia's plant species and 12 percent of its animal species do not occur anywhere else. Colombia has about 1,800 species of birds. That's more than any other country, and represents almost 20 percent of all the bird species in the world.

Opposite: **Tamarins are small monkeys that live in Colombia's forests. They are about the size of squirrels.**

Turtles make their way to the sea during the International Day of the Environment in Camarones.

In the Highlands

Although much of the highlands is now farmland, some areas have been saved as reserves. At El Cocuy and Tamá reserves in the Cordillera Oriental streams, lined with tiny ferns, tumble down through rock-filled valleys. Higher in the mountains are valleys carpeted with grassy slopes and bright flowers. These areas are home to many kinds of birds, including several tiny hummingbirds.

Puracé National Park in the south contains hot springs, milky rivers, and waterfalls. The high slopes of the park's volcano are covered with mosses and lichens. A tangled, moist forest with low trees, bamboo, and ferns blankets the lower slopes. Among the creatures that live in these damp forests are the mountain paca—a rodent as big as a small dog—and the Andean condor, which is extinct in many parts of Colombia. South America's only bear, the spectacled bear, which gets its name from the markings around its eyes, also survives in this remote national park.

Spectacled bears are good climbers. They often build sleeping platforms in trees.

Bringing Back the Condor

Colombia's national bird is the Andean condor, a vulture with an 11-foot (3 m) wingspan. It is one of the world's largest and heaviest birds.

At one time, condors were common in the northern Andes, but they became threatened as humans pushed farther into their habitat and the condors could no longer find enough of their normal food—dead animals. By the 1980s, few condors remained.

Condors are now being raised in captivity and then released into the wild in an effort to increase their population. These efforts have been successful, and Colombia's condor population is slowly growing. Today, more than one hundred of these magnificent birds again soar over the Andes.

Seen from the air, most of the Colombian Andes are green with plant life, but a few areas are dry, even desertlike. The Tatacoa, in the upper Magdalena River valley, is an area of dry forest and eroded rock. Cactuses and other hardy plants dominate the landscape. Lizards and snakes abound today, while the rocks bear fossils of ancient animals.

On the Páramos

Fog often blankets the Andes' higher slopes, an eerie world called the *páramos*. The páramos are dotted with small lakes,

Frailejones are the tallest plants in the páramos. They bloom between October and December, bringing a burst of yellow to the pale green landscape.

boggy areas, and deep gullies. Plants that live in the páramos have adapted to survive both the extreme cold and the intense rays of the Sun. Grasses and hardy shrubs are the most common páramo plants. More striking páramo plants include *frailejones* ("tall friars"), a plant related to the daisy. Some frailejones species grow more than 10 feet (3 m) high. Like many páramo plants, frailejones have a downy covering on their leaves to help protect the plant against the damp cold.

The páramos are also home to some unusual animals, including frogs that carry their eggs on their back and worms almost 5 feet (1.5 m) long. One of the area's largest animals is the rare mountain tapir, a creature that looks something like a pig but is related to the horse and the rhinoceros.

In the Sierra Nevada de Santa Marta

Taking a close look at the Sierra Nevada de Santa Marta, you can see the rich diversity of Colombia's plant and animal life. Where the rainfall is heavy, the forests are thick with tangled vines, tree ferns, and moss-covered trees. These forests often are bathed in mist. In these dense forests, some plants take root on the branches of trees. Many have deep clusters of leaves where rainwater collects. These natural "tanks" provide a home for insect larvae and tiny frogs.

Saving the National Tree—and a Parrot

Colombia's national tree, the wax palm, is native to the Cordillera Central. This magnificent tree reaches heights of about 225 feet (70 m), making it the tallest palm tree in the world.

The fronds of the wax palm were traditionally used by Colombian Catholics in religious processions on Palm Sunday, a week before Easter. Between people felling the palms to harvest the fronds and forestland being cleared to make way for farms, the wax palm became threatened. The decline of the wax palm pushed the yellow-eared parrot to the brink of extinction. These parrots nest only in the wax palm. As the trees disappeared, the number of parrots dropped to just 81.

Something had to be done. Conservation groups and the Catholic Church began working to save both species. The church encouraged Colombians to use other palm species on Palm Sunday. Meanwhile, conservation groups set up a series of nature reserves to protect the areas where the palms still grow. They also planted thousands of wax palms. The program has been an enormous success. By 2006, just five years after the program started, the number of yellow-eared parrots had jumped to 660.

Many brilliantly colored birds live in the Sierra Nevada de Santa Marta, including trogons, curassows, and hummingbirds. Altogether, 628 species of birds have been recorded in this small area. That's about the same as the number found in the United States and Canada combined. Other creatures that live in this range include red howler monkeys, jaguars, sloths, anteaters, and armadillos.

The north and east sides of the Sierra Nevada are dry at lower elevations. The trees there are often spiny. They also have small leaves, which limits water loss. Animals in this dry region include large lizards called iguanas. Shoelace-thin snakes, whose colors blend with the yellowing vines, and huge tortoises also live in the arid Sierra Nevada.

The white-tailed trogon often sits completely still in trees. It eats fruits and insects.

Tayrona National Park lies low in the Sierra Nevada. Its wide beaches are nesting sites for green turtles. These turtles return to the beach where they were born. They come out of the sea at night, scoop out nests, and lay their eggs. Each female turtle of breeding age lays about one hundred eggs up to four times each nesting season.

When the young turtles hatch, they have to make their way back across the beach to the sea. This is a dangerous trip, for they face many predators. On land, creatures such as racoonlike coatis, opossums, and a number of wild cat species prey on the baby turtles. Dogs kept by villagers are another danger, as are birds of prey. It is amazing that any of the young turtles survive!

Tayrona National Park is dotted with white sand beaches and massive boulders.

Oilbirds

Oilbirds feed only on the oily fruit of palm trees. They get their name from the days when indigenous peoples plucked the plump young birds from their nests and melted their fat to use as cooking oil.

Oilbirds nest on ledges in caves. They feed at night. Like bats, they find their way around the caves by echolocation—they make a clicking sound and then judge where objects are from the echoes produced by the clicks. Oilbirds also have a shrieking call, which is deafening in a cave.

The largest oilbird colony in Colombia is in the Cueva de los Guácharos ("Cave of the Oilbirds"), a national park in the Cordillera Oriental. This cave is home to about two thousand oilbirds. The cave floor, which is littered with the remains of palm fruit, provides another special habitat. It is literally crawling with spiders, beetles, and other creatures.

In the Rain Forests

Colombia's thick rain forests are full of life. Birds and butterflies abound. Spider monkeys, howler monkeys, and capuchin monkeys are found in many areas. Smaller primates, such as marmosets and tamarins, are also plentiful. The forest floor is home to countless rodents. Some are small like mice, while others, such as the paca, grow up to 30 inches (76 cm) long.

Lagoons flank many rain forest rivers. These lagoons, which are often covered with giant water lilies, are havens for

Delicate Beauty

Colombia's national flower is a lovely orchid called *Cattleya trianae*. It is named after English botanist William Cattley and Colombian botanist José M. Triana. Orchids have long been prized because they are both delicate and spectacular. About three thousand orchid species grow in Colombia, 10 percent of the total orchid species in existence.

waterbirds, such as herons, egrets, and storks. The rivers are home to many species of fish, including large catfish that can weigh more than 200 pounds (90 kilograms).

Spider monkeys spend most of their life in the highest branches of the rain forest. They almost never come down to the ground.

Every rainy season, the vast Llanos are flooded. After the rains, pools of water remain on the grasslands for months.

La Macarena: Is This the End?

The Sierra de la Macarena is a small range of flat-topped mountains close to the Cordillera Oriental. Its location at the meeting of the Andes Mountains and the Orinoco and Amazon rivers makes it unique. Because the Macarena supports a huge variety of plant and animal species, it was declared a conservation area in 1948.

The Sierra de la Macarena is home to rare creatures like the giant otter, which can reach 7 feet (2 m) long. Threatened deer, giant armadillos, and rodents such as agoutis, pacas (below), and pacaranas also live there.

Not that long ago, only a few local families lived in the Macarena. Then, in the 1980s, loggers, farmers, hunters, and miners moved in. During the 1990s, the Macarena became a center for growing coca, and later it became a rebel stronghold. In 2005, the government permitted spraying over parts of the park to kill the coca. Airplanes swooped over the coca fields, spreading poison. It was the first time that chemicals had been sprayed in a Colombian national park. Experts are uncertain what the future holds for the fragile ecosystem.

Deadly Frogs

Long ago, the peoples of the Chocó forests realized that a tiny colorful frog they called *kokoe* was highly poisonous. Its colors probably evolved as a warning to other animals—a "keep away" signal. These tiny frogs belong to a group known as poison dart frogs. The Chocó peoples hunted by putting poison from the frogs on the tips of blowgun darts. Researchers have since learned that the kokoe's poison is one of the most deadly known to science.

Many types of birds, including tree ducks and herons, gather at these pools, sometimes in large numbers. The rivers and pools are also home to alligator-like caimans. Caimans used to be abundant, but hunting has greatly reduced their number. A large rodent called the capybara lives near the pools and grazes in the grasslands.

Black caimans are the largest predators in the Amazon. They can grow 20 feet (6 m) long.

Land of
El Dorado

HUMANS FIRST SETTLED IN THE AMERICAS SOMETIME between ten thousand and twenty thousand years ago, during the last Ice Age. Sea levels were lower then because much of the world's water was frozen. At the time, a strip of land, that is now covered with water, connected Russia and Alaska. People from Asia simply walked across. Over time, they spread out over North and South America. Some of these people settled in the mountains, valleys, forests, and coastlands that

Opposite: **Bogotá's cathedral stands on Bolívar Plaza. It lies at the heart of the old city.**

Colombians have been farming the slopes of the Cordillera Central for thousands of years.

This golden sculpture was made by the Muisca sometime between the eleventh and the fifteenth century. It was probably intended to be a religious offering.

are now part of Colombia. There, they hunted, fished, and gathered nuts and seeds to survive. Between three thousand and four thousand years ago, they began to grow corn and other crops. They also began to settle in villages and develop organized societies.

Native Peoples

When the Spaniards arrived in the region early in the sixteenth century, they found various groups living in what is now Colombia. The Muisca, also known as the Chibcha, made up about one-third of Colombia's indigenous population. They lived on the plain where Bogotá now sits. The Tairona lived in the highlands near the Caribbean coast, while the Sinú were in the lower Magdalena River valley. The Tumaco settled on the Pacific Coast. Most of the other peoples, including the Quimbaya, Tolima, and Calima, lived in the central and southern highlands.

The Muisca lived in villages of thatched wooden huts. They grew corn, potatoes, beans, and squash. Their tools were simple wooden digging sticks and spades. The Muisca grew different crops at different levels of the mountain slopes. Potatoes, for example, grow well on cooler, high slopes, while corn and fruit grow better on lower levels. Generally, the Muisca

A Trip to the Past

Hundreds of stone figures rise from the ground at San Agustín, an archaeological site near Popayán. Many of the statues represent gods that are part human and part animal. Some have big, round eyes, while the eyes of others are long, narrow slits. Statues depict sacred animals such as the eagle, a symbol of power and light, and the frog, which is associated with water. Others show a jaguar or a catlike figure with large fangs. Some of the statues are two thousand years old.

Not far from San Agustín is Tierradentro, a site with a hundred underground burial chambers carved out of rock. Staircases built into the rock lead to the burial vaults. Several vaults have domelike ceilings supported by huge rock pillars.

wore simple clothing, such as white cotton tunics or short pants and shirts, and went barefoot.

Other native peoples had lifestyles similar to the Muisca's, though there were some differences. The Sinú built large huts in which many families lived together, while the Quimbaya lived in small groups. Almost all the native Colombians worshipped the Sun, the Moon, and other natural forces as gods and made offerings to them.

The Legend of El Dorado

The ceremony of El Dorado, "The Golden One," took place when the Muisca gained a new ruler. He was taken to Lake Guatavita, where a raft was prepared with offerings for the gods. He was stripped of his clothes and covered from head to toe in fine gold dust. His nobles, wearing their finest clothes and jewelry, joined him on the raft with heaps of gold and emeralds. The raft left the shore to the sound of trumpets and flutes. In the middle of the lake, the chief and his nobles threw all the gold, emeralds, and other treasures into the water. Then the chief dived in to the lake to remove the gold dust from his skin.

Rumors of a lake filled with gold reached the Spanish when they arrived in South America. They tried many ways to drain the lake of water and find the gold.

People today continue to try, using modern equipment. No one has succeeded.

Colombia's native peoples were skilled potters and goldsmiths. Much of the gold came from riverbeds, though some was dug from deep shafts in the mountains. In areas without gold, the Indians traded fish, salt, and cloth for the precious metal.

Searching for Gold

Spanish explorers reached Colombia's Caribbean coast in 1500, but serious attempts to settle the region did not begin until several years later. Santa Marta, the first permanent Spanish settlement in South America, was founded in 1525. Soon, rumors of gold and other treasure prompted the Spaniards to journey into the interior.

In 1536, Gonzalo Jiménez de Quesada led an expedition of about 650 men across South America. He was probably trying to reach the kingdom of the Inca, a people in Peru known to have great wealth. Jiménez de Quesada pushed up the Magdalena River through swamps infested with alligators and snakes. His soldiers were starving, but he kept on. Somewhere along the route, perhaps having heard of rich salt mines, emeralds, and the legend of El Dorado, he abandoned the river. He and his party then climbed the Cordillera Oriental and arrived in the land of the Muisca. Only 166 of his men survived the journey.

In 1535, Gonzalo Jiménez de Quesada traveled from Spain to South America to become a judge in Santa Marta. The following year, he was sent on his expedition across Colombia.

At the time, the Muisca were divided into clans headed by the Zipa and the Zaque, who were at war with each other. This helped Jiménez de Quesada conquer the territory. He looted the royal capital of the Zaque, taking 150,000 pesos of gold and 230 emeralds. Jiménez de Quesada went on to found Santa Fe de Bogotá in 1538.

Meanwhile, another expedition was approaching Muisca territory from the east. Nikolaus Federmann, a German, headed out of Venezuela across the vast grasslands toward the Andes in 1537. In forty days, he climbed from near sea level to a height of more than 11,500 feet (3,500 m). It was intensely cold, and about half of his men died on the way. Eventually, he reached Muisca territory, only to find that Jiménez de Quesada had arrived there first.

Sebastián de Belalcázar served in Peru during the Spanish conquest of the Incas. After receiving his share of the Inca treasure, Belalcázar headed north to Ecuador. There, the story goes, he heard about El Dorado and decided to push on to find the lake filled with gold. On his way, he founded the towns of Cali and Popayán in southern Colombia.

The leaders of the three expeditions unexpectedly met up in the land of the Muisca. They did not fight one another. Instead, they came to an agreement that led the Spanish monarchy to create the Audiencia of Santa Fe de Bogotá in 1549. The audiencia was a kind of council that managed the affairs of Colombia. It was under the control of the Viceroyalty of Peru, a Spanish colony to the south.

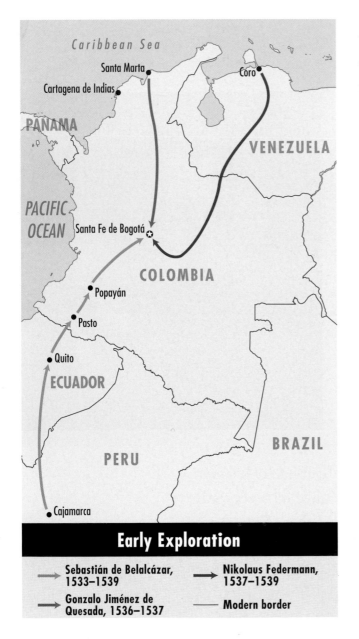

Early Exploration

→ Sebastián de Belalcázar, 1533–1539

→ Gonzalo Jiménez de Quesada, 1536–1537

→ Nikolaus Federmann, 1537–1539

— Modern border

Life in the Colony

The new colony provided the Spaniards with fertile land and a wealth of minerals, including gold, emeralds, and salt. The newcomers treated the indigenous peoples cruelly. They forced them to work in slavelike conditions and made them pay a tribute, or tax, to the Spanish crown. Many native people died of diseases brought by the Spaniards, such as smallpox and influenza. The native peoples had never before been exposed to these diseases, so their bodies could not fight them.

During the sixteenth century, black African slaves were imported to work on the region's sugar plantations and in mines. Gradually, the racial mix of the population changed. But Spaniards kept all the power. Those born in Spain were known as *peninsulares*, while Spaniards born in the colony were called *criollos*.

Cartagena and the Pirates

The city of Cartagena de Indias, which is often called simply Cartagena, lies on Colombia's northern coast. Founded in 1533, it soon became the colony's principal port. Ships bearing gold, silver, and other treasure from all over South America sailed from Cartagena for Europe. The ships were heavily guarded, and the city faced frequent attacks from pirates.

The French pirates Jean and Martin Cote raided Cartagena in 1560, and in 1586, Englishman Sir Francis Drake inflicted heavy damage. With 1,300 men, Drake captured the city, looted it, burned down some 200 houses, and destroyed the half-finished cathedral. He then made off with 110,000 gold ducats.

The people of Cartagena tried to defend themselves. They built a series of forts and surrounded the town with a wall 39 feet (12 m) high and 56 feet (17 m) thick. Nevertheless, French admiral Baron de Pointis, with ten thousand men, beat down the defenses in 1697 and ravaged the city.

By 1741, Great Britain and Spain were at war, and Cartagena came under attack not by pirates but by the British navy. Admiral Edward Vernon surrounded the city with nine thousand troops and 186 warships for six weeks. Vernon sent

Cartagena

Cartagena is perhaps Colombia's most beautiful and historic city. Thick walls still surround the old city. A yellow clock tower stands above the main gate, and beyond is the Plaza de los Coches ("Square of the Carriages"). In this square, slaves were bought and sold when they first arrived from Africa.

Nearby is the church of San Pedro Claver, named after a monk who devoted his life to caring for the slaves. Cartagena's cathedral stands on one corner of the Plaza Bolívar. It is not far from the Palace of the Inquisition, a notorious place where Spanish priests used dreadful punishment to subdue people of other faiths. Many other churches grace the city, and fine mansions and houses with balconies line its streets.

Outside the city walls stands the great fort of San Felipe, complete with battlements, terraces, and guard-houses. A statue of Blas de Lezo, who helped fend off the British in 1741, guards the fort.

In 1741, the English surrounded the city of Cartagena for weeks before they finally attacked it. Many soldiers fell ill during the assault, however, and the English were not able to get past the fort of San Felipe.

word to England that the attack was successful. But he had bragged too quickly. The Cartagenians, led by the one-eyed, one-legged, one-armed Blas de Lezo, fought off the attack and captured some two thousand British troops.

Rebellion

In 1717, the Spanish crown created a large colony called the Viceroyalty of New Granada. Santa Fe de Bogotá was its capital. The viceroyalty included what are now the countries of Colombia, Panama, Venezuela, and Ecuador.

During the eighteenth century, people in the colony grew increasingly resentful toward the Spanish authorities. They were unhappy paying taxes to the Spanish crown. Spain also forbade the colonies from trading with any other country. The criollos particularly resented this. Many of them were involved in trade because the peninsulares excluded them from most government posts.

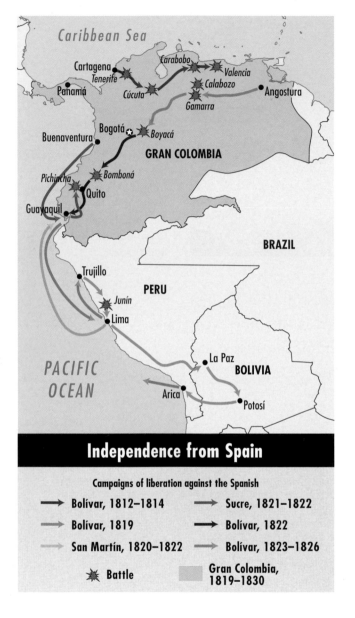

Caribbean Sea

Cartagena
Tenerife
Carabobo
Valencia
Calabozo
Panamá
Cúcuta
Gamarra
Angostura
Bogotá
Boyacá
GRAN COLOMBIA
Buenaventura
Bomboná
Pichincha
Quito
Guayaquil
BRAZIL
Trujillo
PERU
Junín
Lima
La Paz
PACIFIC
OCEAN
BOLIVIA
Arica
Potosí

Independence from Spain

Campaigns of liberation against the Spanish

→ Bolívar, 1812–1814   → Sucre, 1821–1822

→ Bolívar, 1819   → Bolívar, 1822

→ San Martín, 1820–1822   → Bolívar, 1823–1826

✳ Battle   Gran Colombia, 1819–1830

New Granada's first rebellion against the Spanish crown occurred in 1781. It was brutally crushed. But the spirit of rebellion was kept alive when Antonio Nariño translated Thomas Paine's pamphlet *The Rights of Man* in 1794. In this work, Paine defended the French Revolution and encouraged the English to overthrow their monarchy and form a republic.

Independence

In the early 1800s, Europe was ravaged by war. With Spain paying little attention to its colonies in the Americas, the colonists in New Granada set up an independent government in 1810.

They disagreed about how best to run the colony, however. The Centralists wanted power to be concentrated in Bogotá, while the Federalists wanted more power for the provinces. This disagreement resulted in civil war.

In 1814, Spain once again turned its attention to the colonies. Spanish troops soon arrived in the region, and the civil war made it easier for them to regain control. Afterward, they executed hundreds of people and destroyed the countryside. This only increased the colonists' determination to gain independence.

Federalist troops escaped into the Llanos. They regrouped under General Francisco de Paula Santander and joined forces with Simón Bolívar, a Venezuelan general leading the fight for independence. Bolívar had assembled an army of tough, fearless horsemen from the Llanos.

In May 1819, Bolívar and his men began a march from the Venezuelan plains across the cold, windswept cordilleras to Bogotá. There, on August 7, 1819, they defeated the Spanish forces at the Battle of Boyacá, and Colombia became independent.

Gran Colombia

After the victory, disagreements continued between the Centralists, supported by Bolívar, and the Federalists, led by Santander. Bolívar won, and in 1821 the new state of Gran Colombia was created with Bolívar as president and Santander as vice president. The new state was made up of what are now Venezuela, Colombia, Panama, and Ecuador. Despite being president, Bolívar left almost immediately to help Peru gain its independence.

It soon became clear that Gran Colombia was so large that it was almost impossible to govern. By 1830,

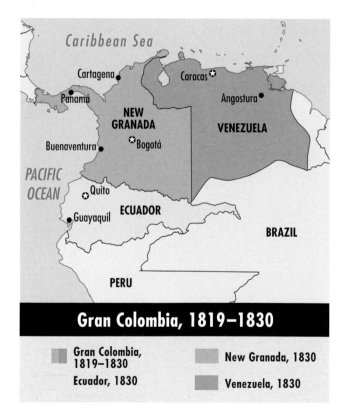

Gran Colombia, 1819–1830

■ Gran Colombia, 1819–1830   ■ New Granada, 1830
■ Ecuador, 1830   ■ Venezuela, 1830

Francisco de Paula Santander

Francisco de Paula Santander was born in 1792. He studied law and then entered the military at age eighteen, quickly rising through the ranks. By age twenty, Santander was at the center of the fight for Colombia's independence. He fought alongside Simón Bolívar at the Battle of Boyacá. In 1821, when he was just twenty-eight years old, he was elected vice president of New Granada.

Though he often served as president when Bolívar was absent, the two men disagreed on how to govern the country. When someone tried to kill Bolívar in 1828, Santander was blamed. He was at first sentenced to death but was then exiled instead. Bolívar died in 1830, the same year Gran Colombia broke up.

Santander was invited back and served as president of New Granada from 1832 to 1837. He died in Bogotá in 1840.

the country was split up. Colombia became the Republic of New Granada. Its name was changed to Colombia in 1863.

> ### Conservatives and Liberals

The Centralists and the Federalists became known as the Conservatives and the Liberals. The Conservatives were supported by the powerful Catholic Church. The Liberals wanted to reduce the church's power. They also called for social reforms that included abolishing slavery and helping the poor.

The Conservatives agreed with some of the reforms, but for most of the nineteenth century Colombia experienced violent conflict as the two sides squabbled. In 1899, a Liberal revolt turned into the War of a Thousand Days, which lasted until 1902. In this civil war, almost one hundred thousand people died, out of a population of only four million.

The Panama Canal

In the early twentieth century, the region that is now Panama was part of Colombia. Though remote, Panama was important because it was the narrowest land crossing from the Atlantic to the Pacific. If a canal was built across Panama, ships traveling from one ocean to the other would no longer have to make the long journey around the distant southern tip of South America.

France was the first country to try to build a canal in Panama, but the effort failed. The United States was also interested in building a canal. The United States agreed to support Panama in its fight for independence from Colombia in return for the right to construct the Panama Canal and to control the area known as the Panama Canal Zone.

Panama became independent in 1903, and the first ship passed through the Panama Canal in 1914. Colombia did not accept the situation until 1921, when the United States softened the blow with a payment of US$25 million. The United States returned the canal to Panama's control in 1999.

The Conservatives held power in Colombia until 1930. During that time, the country prospered, the coffee and banana industries developed, and oil was discovered. But nothing was done to help the poor. When the Liberals returned to power, the poor were their first priority. In the 1930s, Liberal president Alfonso López Pumarejo paid particular attention to education and health care for the poor.

In 1948, Liberal leader Jorge Eliécer Gaitán was killed. His death unleashed an explosion of violence in Colombia. Angry citizens looted the capital. Many of its buildings were damaged or destroyed. The violence then spread to the countryside. *La Violencia* ("The Violence"), as it became known, lasted from about 1948 to 1962. As many as two hundred thousand people died in this civil war.

Jorge Eliécer Gaitán

Jorge Eliécer Gaitán (1903–1948) is a hero to many Colombians. He was the son of a bookseller and a teacher, and his family did not have a lot of money. Still, he got a good education, earned a law degree, and became a professor at the National University. Gaitán was involved in politics from the age of sixteen. He became a national figure seven years later, defending the rights of striking banana workers fired on by the army. Gaitán had a huge following among the poor and deprived. He became mayor of Bogotá in 1936, minister of education in 1940, labor minister in 1943, and chief of the Colombian Liberal Party in 1947. Then, in 1948, he was assassinated by Juan Roa Sierra. No one knows why, because Roa Sierra was in turn killed by an angry mob.

The National Front

To help bring peace to Colombia, the Liberals and Conservatives decided to share power. In 1958, they created what is known as the National Front, agreeing that they would alternate in the presidency every four years until 1974. Congress and all other government and cabinet posts would be equally split between the two parties.

Guillermo León Valencia served as president from 1962 to 1966. His father was a respected poet and translator, as well as a politician.

The first National Front president was a Liberal, Alberto Lleras Camargo. He was an internationally respected politician and diplomat. He was followed in 1962 by a Conservative, Guillermo León Valencia, who in turn was followed by the Liberal Carlos Lleras Restrepo.

The National Front ended in 1974, having brought the country some peace and economic improvement. During its years, Colombia moved from an agricultural to an industrial economy.

Rebel Groups

In the years after La Violencia, rebel groups fighting the government became a major threat. The Revolutionary Armed Forces of Colombia (known as FARC, after its initials in Spanish) and the Army of National Liberation (known as ELN) emerged in the 1960s. The April 19 Movement, or M-19, arose in the early 1970s.

By the end of the 1970s, perhaps a dozen different rebel groups controlled many rural towns and villages, though they had little presence in the cities. In 1982, in the face of mounting fighting, President Belisario Betancur said the rebels would not be prosecuted if they agreed to lay down their arms.

Some accepted his offer, and the FARC formed their own political party, the Unión Patriótica (UP). But the peace did not last. The UP became a target for deadly right-wing groups, while other rebels continued much as before, with frequent bombings and murders.

The Drug Trade

In the 1970s, the drug trade became hugely profitable in Colombia. Drug dealers such as Pablo Escobar of Medellín gained enormous wealth and power. Escobar had many supporters among the poor because he helped them with housing and donated large sums of money to charity. But to the government, he was a threat. He kept a private army of hundreds of young men who murdered anyone who opposed him, including judges and politicians.

Three presidential candidates were assassinated during the 1990 election, prompting President Virgilio Barco Vargas to call for an all-out war on drugs. Still, violence continued to increase. Car bombs killed hundreds. Security buildings and police were targeted. In one incident, more than one hundred people died when an airplane was blown up.

After César Gaviria Trujillo became president in 1990, he offered the drug traffickers short sentences in return for their surrender and cooperation. His approach appeared to be successful when Escobar and others gave themselves up. It did not stop the drug trade, however. Escobar continued to run his business with computers, faxes, and phones from considerable luxury in prison.

Then, one day in July 1992, Escobar escaped from prison. Everyone was outraged that this had been allowed to happen. The Colombian government now insisted that Escobar must be captured or killed at all costs. In December 1993, a phone call he made to his family was traced to a house in Medellín. He was killed while trying to escape.

Pablo Escobar made a fortune as a drug dealer. In 1989, *Forbes* magazine said he was the seventh-richest man in the world.

Elections in 1994 demonstrated just how much control the rebels had in the countryside. Candidates were often unable to campaign, and voters were intimidated. As a result, many people with links to the rebels or drug dealers were elected mayors or town councillors.

In 1999, President Andrés Pastrana Arango introduced Plan Colombia, which aimed to end armed conflict, stifle the drug trade, and tackle the country's basic social and economic problems. Pastrana received considerable international support for his plan, but some aspects of it were controversial.

Andrés Pastrana Arango was president from 1998 to 2002. His father, Misael Pastrana Borrero, had been president in the 1970s.

FARC is one of the most powerful rebel groups in the world. It has between twelve thousand and eighteen thousand members.

For example, the plan used chemical sprays to kill coca crops, which some thought presented a health hazard in rural areas. The United States was by far the largest donor under Plan Colombia. Most U.S. aid was directed toward the military and the antidrug program rather than the plan's economic and social programs. This also angered some people.

Álvaro Uribe Vélez, who was elected president in 2002, continued working on Plan Colombia. He achieved considerable success. Some rebel groups agreed to stop fighting, while others gave up their weapons. The ELN and FARC no longer wield the power they once did. Uribe was reelected in 2006, as the people of Colombia gave his policies a vote of confidence. The election took place without any major violence, which was, perhaps, the most hopeful sign of all.

Governing Colombia

I N 1990, THE PEOPLE OF COLOMBIA VOTED IN FAVOR OF A Constitutional Assembly that would rewrite the country's constitution. The old constitution, which dated from 1886, was the oldest in South America. It no longer met the needs of the people. It was time for Colombia to modernize its political system.

Representatives to the Constitutional Assembly were elected. They came from every section of society. There were former rebels, indigenous people, and Protestants, as well as members of the traditional Conservative and Liberal parties. The assembly produced a constitution that gave these minority groups representation in Congress for the first time.

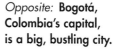
Opposite: **Bogotá, Colombia's capital, is a big, bustling city.**

Members of Colombia's legislature gathered in 2002 to watch Álvaro Uribe Vélez be sworn in as president.

The National Flag

Colombia's flag consists of three horizontal stripes—yellow, dark blue, and red. The yellow stripe represents the wealth of the nation, the red stripe stands for the blood shed for independence, and the blue stripe in the middle is for the Atlantic and Pacific Oceans and Colombia's rivers.

The National Government

Colombia's government has three branches: executive, legislative, and judicial. The head of the executive branch is the president, who is elected to a four-year term. In 2005, the constitution was changed to allow the president to serve two

NATIONAL GOVERNMENT OF COLOMBIA

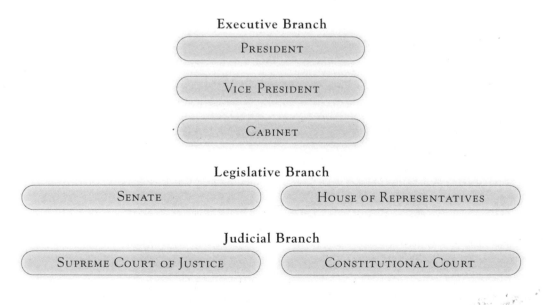

Executive Branch

PRESIDENT

VICE PRESIDENT

CABINET

Legislative Branch

SENATE   HOUSE OF REPRESENTATIVES

Judicial Branch

SUPREME COURT OF JUSTICE   CONSTITUTIONAL COURT

four-year terms in a row. The president is assisted by a vice president and a cabinet of ministers.

The legislature consists of two parts, the Senate and the House of Representatives. Members of both houses serve four-year terms. The Senate has 100 members, and the House of Representatives has 165 members. The legislature includes designated seats for minority groups. Indigenous people have two seats in the Senate, and blacks and former rebels have two seats each in the House of Representatives.

The National Capitol houses both the Senate and the House of Representatives. It was built between 1847 and 1926.

Carlos Lleras Restrepo

When Carlos Lleras Restrepo died in 1994 at age eighty-six, he was Colombia's most respected elder statesman. He had been a leading member of the Liberal Party since the 1930s and served as president from 1966 to 1970. His presidency coincided with the National Front period.

The low point of his career was the accusation of fraudulent elections in 1970, which led to the formation of the M-19 rebels. They took their name, Movimiento 19 de Abril, from the date of the election, April 19. After he retired from politics, Lleras Restrepo worked on a history of Colombia. Though he had written twelve volumes before he died, the work was unfinished.

The judicial branch consists of Colombia's legal system. It is headed by the Supreme Court of Justice, which is the highest court on all matters of criminal law. Judges serve one eight-year term. They cannot be appointed for a second term. Other courts include the Constitutional Court, which rules on matters relating to the constitution, and the State Council, which is the highest court for cases concerning the administration

The Supreme Court meets in the Palace of Justice.

of the government. The judicial system also includes district courts and provincial and municipal judges.

Provincial Government

Colombia is divided into thirty-two departments and the Capital District. Departments are similar to states or provinces. The people in each department elect a governor and a legislature for that department. The departments are divided into about 1,100 municipalities. The municipalities, including the Capital District of Bogotá, are headed by mayors.

The National Anthem

"Himno Nacional de la República de Colombia" ("National Anthem of the Republic of Colombia") is the official title of Colombia's national anthem. Oreste Sindici, an Italian-born Colombian, wrote the music for it in 1887. The words come from a poem by President Rafael Núñez, "¡Oh! Gloria Inmarcesible!" ("Oh Unfading Glory!"). The anthem was adopted in 1920.

Spanish lyrics

CHORUS:
¡Oh gloria inmarcesible!
Oh jubilo inmortal
en surcos de Dolores
el bien germina ya.

Cesó la horrible noche
la libertad sublime
derrama las auroras
de su invencible luz.
La humanidad entera,
que entre cadenas gime
comprende las palabras
del que murió en la Cruz.

English lyrics

CHORUS:
Oh unfading glory!
Oh immortal joy
In furrows of sorrow
Good now grows.

The dreadful night is over
Sublime freedom
Scatters the auroras
Of its invincible light
The whole of humanity
In chains wailing
Understands the words
Of He who died on the cross.

Bogotá: Did You Know This?

Bogotá was founded in 1538 by Gonzalo Jiménez de Quesada. He named the settlement Santa Fe de Bacatá after his home town of Santa Fe in Spain and the Muisca settlement Bacatá. By the early eighteenth century, when the city was the capital of the Viceroyalty of New Granada, Bacatá had become Bogotá.

Bogotá is on a high plain in the Cordillera Oriental. Because of its high altitude, the city has a springlike climate for most of the year. The average daily temperature in January is 58°F (14.5°C) and in July is 57°F (14°C).

Bogotá is by far Colombia's largest city, with a population of about seven million. It is also the hub of the country's cultural, educational, financial, and political life. Bogotá has many parks where people can relax, children can play games, and free concerts are given. Bogotá also has a modern transportation system and one of the longest bike-path networks of any city in the world, covering some 187 miles (300 km).

to Canadian Embassy
Church of San Diego
Santamaría Bullring
District Planetarium
Independence Park
Olaya Herrera National Park
Sunday Flea Market
Museum of Modern Art
to American Embassy
National Library
BOSQUE IZQUIERDO
Ecotourism Office
Las Nieves Church
LA PAZ
LA CAPUCHINA
Tercera Church
VERACRUZ
Veracruz Church
Santander Park
San Francisco Church
Gold Museum
Las Aguas Church
University of the Andes
Periodistas Park
Concepción Church
Justice Palace
July 20 Museum
LA CONCORDIA
Liévano Building
Bolívar Plaza
Primada Cathedral
Luis Ángel Arango Library
National Capitol
San Carlos Palace
Candelaria Church
Santa Clara Church
Botero Collection
Colonial Art Museum
Military Museum
House of Nariño
LA CANDELARIA

0   200 yards
0   200 meters

Bogotá

Emeralds
and Energy

70

FOR CENTURIES, COLOMBIA'S ECONOMY WAS BASED ON agriculture, and from the nineteenth century on, especially coffee. Today, Colombia is third only to Brazil and Vietnam as a world coffee producer. Colombia is also rich in mineral and energy resources, and industry now contributes more to the economy than agriculture.

The effects of drug money on the Colombian economy are hard to determine. Many experts believe that the drugs shipped from Colombia are worth more than all the country's other exports combined.

Opposite: **The fruit of the cacao tree are filled with seeds that are used to make chocolate.**

A worker picks coffee beans on a farm near Bogotá.

Political violence and the drug trade have disrupted development in Colombia, hurting the legal economy. In recent years, however, the economy has improved. Still, about 11 percent of workers are without jobs, and almost half the population lives below the poverty line.

Agriculture

Coffee was introduced into Colombia as early as 1700 and developed into an important industry in the nineteenth century. The industry really took off about 1910, when railroads were built to take the coffee from where it is grown in the Cordillera Central to the ports.

Colombia has an estimated half million coffee farms. The average farm covers less than 4 acres (1.5 hectares).

Today, much of the coffee is produced by small family farms. The finest coffee grows on hilly slopes at elevations of 3,000 to 6,000 feet (900 to 1,800 m). The mountain climate is ideal for the arabica plant, a mild variety of coffee that traditionally thrives in the shade. Coffee farmers also plant varieties that do well in open sunlight. It is hard to use machines on the hillsides, so many farmers use traditional tools—the hoe and the machete—and pick the coffee beans by hand. At harvest time, the whole family pitches in. A mature tree produces about two thousand beans a year. When processed, this fills only a 1-pound (0.5 kg) coffee can. An experienced farmer can pick about 200 pounds (90 kg) of coffee a day.

The farmers use machines to separate the beans from the outer pulp, and the beans are then washed and dried in the sun. Since there are few good roads around small coffee farms, the beans are carried by mule and donkey to the nearest mill. There, they are checked and bagged for export.

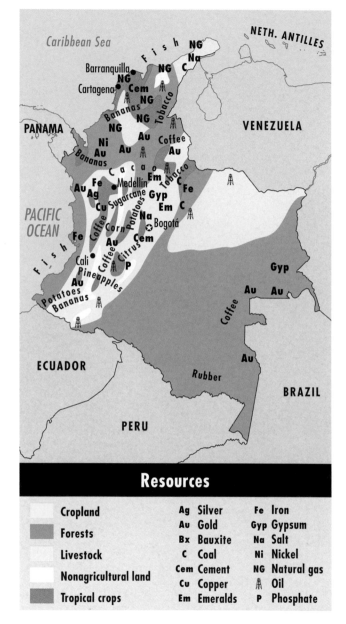

Resources

Cropland	Ag	Silver	Fe	Iron
Forests	Au	Gold	Gyp	Gypsum
Livestock	Bx	Bauxite	Na	Salt
Nonagricultural land	C	Coal	Ni	Nickel
Tropical crops	Cem	Cement	NG	Natural gas
	Cu	Copper	⚒	Oil
	Em	Emeralds	P	Phosphate

A man transports bundles of sugarcane by horse. Most of Colombia's sugarcane is grown in the Cauca River valley.

In recent years, Colombia's coffee industry has suffered. World prices for coffee have dropped, and disease has hit about half of the country's coffee bushes. Many growers are now in debt and seek government help.

With its varied climate, Colombia also produces many other crops. Sugarcane is grown mainly in river valleys and on the Pacific coast. Bananas grow on the Caribbean coast. Potatoes, corn, and cacao, which is used to make chocolate, are also important products.

Outside Bogotá, greenhouses for the cut-flower industry cover acres of land. This industry took off in Colombia in the 1970s. Today, the nation is one of the world's leading exporters of roses, carnations, chrysanthemums, and orchids. Medellín claims to be the world center for orchids, and its flowers are flown to the United States every day.

Colombia produces more than 60 percent of all the cut flowers sold in the United States.

Forestry, Ranching, and Fishing

About half of Colombia is covered by forests. Into the second half of the twentieth century, few roads passed through the country's wooded areas, so the timber industry was slow to take off. Once roads were built, vast tracts of forests were cut, and logs were floated on rivers or sent by truck to sawmills.

Some forests were cleared to make way for cattle ranches and farms. Cattle are also raised in the Llanos, in the river valleys, and on the Caribbean coast. At times, Colombia has had nearly as many cattle as people. The cattle provide both beef

Cowboys herd cattle in the Llanos. There are about twenty-five million cattle in Colombia.

Money Facts

Colombia's currency is called the peso. Money is issued in bills valued at 1,000, 2,000, 5,000, 10,000, and 20,000 pesos, and in coins valued at 50, 100, 200, 500, and 1,000 pesos. In 2007, US$1 equaled 2,235 pesos. Most of Colombia's paper money shows important figures from history. For example, the 5,000-peso note has an image of General Francisco de Paula Santander, a leader of the war for independence.

and leather. The leather is turned into fashionable handbags and luggage for people in Europe and North America.

Though Colombia has a long coastline and many rivers, its fishing industry is small. The most successful commercial fishing effort is shrimp farms, which are located on the Caribbean coast.

A fisherman casts a net off Salamanca Island.

Emeralds and Energy **77**

Huge ships dock at Buenaventura, Colombia's main port on the Pacific Ocean. The United States is Colombia's biggest trading partner.

In 2005, industry accounted for about one-third of Colombia's gross domestic product, the total value of the goods and services produced in the country. Colombia's four major industrial centers are Bogotá, Medellín, Cali, and Barranquilla. The nation's factories manufacture tires, processed food and drinks, transportation equipment, chemical products, medicines, cement, and iron and steel products.

What Colombia Grows, Makes, and Mines

Agriculture (2003)

Sugarcane	37,000,000 metric tons
Potatoes	2,872,000 metric tons
Plantains	2,911,000 metric tons
Coffee	703,000 metric tons

Manufacturing (2004, value in Colombian pesos)

Processed food and beverages	11,194,820,965
Petroleum products	5,337,918,506
Chemical products	4,619,612,739

Mining (2004)

Coal	53,693,000 metric tons
Emeralds	9,820,000 carats
Iron ore	642,546,000 metric tons

Colombia's mineral deposits include nickel, gold, silver, platinum, copper, bauxite, iron ore, phosphates, uranium, rock salt, marble, and limestone. The country is also rich in emeralds, a highly prized green gemstone. Most of Colombia's emeralds come from the Muzo and Chivor mines in the mountains near Bogotá. Colombia produces about 60 percent of the world's total supply of emeralds.

Ordinary people often dig for emeralds in small mines or hunt for them in rivers. Men, women, and children live crowded into tin shacks on mountain slopes, mostly without

Men search for emeralds in a riverbed in Muzo.

running water or electricity, and spend their lives searching for the precious stones. If they are lucky enough to find some, they sell the emeralds to local traders, who then sell them again to someone who puts them on the international market for shaping into jewelry. In 1920, the world's largest emerald, the 632-carat Patricia, was found in Colombia.

Much of Colombia's gold comes from the northwest. Many poor people search for gold in rivers. They live and work in grim conditions in the hope that one day they will strike it rich.

The Green War

In the 1970s, Colombia's drug cartels decided to take over the emerald market. But the bosses of the emerald industry had other ideas. In the 1980s, the mines became the center of a bloody war. Up to three thousand people died before the drug cartels recognized that they could not control the gem trade.

The man who did more than anyone to resist the cartels was Victor Carranza. Carranza was born into poverty, but over the course of his life he became one of Colombia's richest men. He owns two of the world's top emerald companies.

In the mid-1990s, Carranza forged a peace deal with the drug cartels. But he was then charged with financing violent right-wing groups and imprisoned. Carranza was released from jail in 2002.

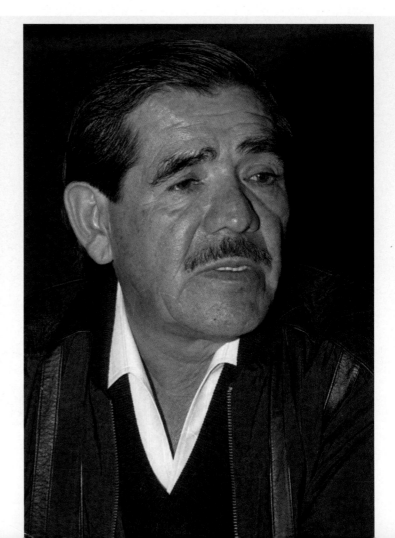

A man moves barrels of oil at a factory in Colombia. Colombia produces about a half million barrels of oil a day.

Energy

Oil is Colombia's top export, accounting for about one-quarter of all export earnings. But oil exports have declined in recent years. Experts believe Colombia may have to import oil if it does not develop more of its reserves.

Colombia's oil reserves are thought to be huge. The most recent oil discoveries have been in the Llanos. In the 1990s, one of the biggest oilfields in the world was found there.

The terrorist activities of the FARC and the ELN have deterred companies from investing in the oil business. The ELN has consistently bombed oil pipelines. The Caño Limón pipeline, which carries oil for almost 500 miles (800 km) to the Caribbean coast, was bombed a record 170 times in 2001 and more than 1,000 times in all.

Weights and Measures

Colombia uses a mixed system of weights and measures. The metric system was introduced in 1857, but Colombians generally use traditional Spanish weights and measures. In this system, basic units include the *vara* (about 28 inches, or 71 cm), the *libra* (about 1 pound, or 0.45 kg), and the *arroba* (about 25 pounds, or 11.3 kg). Colombians measure gasoline in U.S. gallons.

Colombia has the largest coal deposits in Latin America. The nation's richest coalfield is the huge mining complex of Carbones del Cerrejón in the Guajira Peninsula. The high-quality hard coal is near the surface and easily mined.

Colombia has a rich supply of natural gas, which is often found near oil deposits. Gas reserves have also been located in the Guajira Peninsula.

Transportation

It's not easy to travel across the Andes. To cope with mountain slopes, roads often zigzag uphill, and many bridges are needed to cross rivers. Landslides are a constant hazard. Only about 15 percent of the nation's roads are paved.

In cities, people use buses and cars, and Medellín has a subway system. Brightly painted open-sided buses called *chivas* operate on the Caribbean coast and between some highland towns. Inside the chivas are wooden benches. Every bit of space on the bus is used for people and bundles, including the roof.

Colombia's main airline, Avianca, was established in 1919, making it one of the oldest airlines in South America. With airplanes, getting from one side of Colombia to the other is no

problem. Bogotá's El Dorado Airport is the hub of the system, but there are airports in even the most remote areas of the country.

Barranquilla, on the Caribbean coast, and Buenaventura, on the Pacific, are Colombia's principal ports. Riverboats are often the only way to get about in the Amazon and Chocó regions.

Colombia has 101 airports with paved runways.

No Rules

A Colombian will tell you that driving in Colombia is almost a sport. Even basic traffic rules are not respected. There are no particular driving customs, and not much courtesy, logic, or common sense, either. Speed limits in Colombia are unusually low: just 37 miles (60 km) per hour on the highway, 19 miles (30 km) per hour in the city, and 25 miles (40 km) per hour on roads outside the cities. But no one pays attention to these limits, and the police do not fine people for speeding.

The Faces
of Colombia

Persons per square mile		Persons per square kilometer	
260–517		100–200	
130–259		50–99	
65–129		25–49	
25–64		10–24	
3–24		1–9	
fewer than 3		fewer than 1	

S EVERAL DECADES AGO, PEOPLE living in rural Colombia started moving to the cities in large numbers. They wanted to escape the widespread violence in the countryside and find better lives for themselves and their families. In 1938, only about one-third of Colombians lived in cities. Today, three-quarters of Colombians are urban dwellers. More than 80 percent of the people in Colombia live in the highlands.

Nearly forty-four million people live in Colombia. That makes Colombia the fourth most populous country in the Western Hemisphere, after the United States, Brazil, and Mexico. More than half of Colombians are *mestizos*, the mixed-race descendants of indigenous people and Europeans. The next-largest group is whites, who are mainly the descendants of Spanish settlers or other European immigrants. Blacks and mulattos—people of mixed African and European parentage—together account for about 18 percent of the population. Two small groups make up

Opposite: **A Wayuu man from the Guajira Peninsula**

Most Colombians have both European and indigenous roots.

the remainder: *zambos*, who are people with mixed African and indigenous backgrounds, and the last surviving indigenous peoples, who make up no more than 1 percent of the population.

Mestizos and Whites

Mestizos form the bulk of the middle and working classes. Most whites have lighter skin than mestizos.

Relatively few immigrants came to Colombia compared with other major South American countries. Most were Spanish colonists, but a small number of other Europeans immigrated during the nineteenth and twentieth centuries. They included Dutch, German, French, Swiss, Belgian, and, in smaller numbers, Polish, Lithuanian, English, and Croatian people.

Who Lives in Colombia?	
Mestizos	58%
Whites	20%
Mulattoes	14%
Blacks	4%
Zambos	3%
Indigenous peoples	1%

Afro-Colombians

Afro-Colombians are blacks and mulattos descended from African slaves. Traditionally, most Afro-Colombians settled along the coasts, in the Chocó region, and in the Magdalena and Cauca river valleys, where they worked on sugarcane or banana plantations, on cattle ranches, and in gold mines. Most lived in poverty and had few prospects.

During the 1970s, many black people left their rural homes for urban areas in search of new economic and social opportunities for their children. They did not find them. Instead, they joined the ranks of the urban poor, living on the edge of big cities in places with high levels of poverty and violence.

Less than half of Afro-Colombian teenagers go to high school. Most Afro-Colombians find work as domestic servants, in the construction industry, or as street vendors. Few make it to the top jobs in government, business, the armed forces, or medicine.

Native Colombians

Some fifty different indigenous groups live in Colombia. Together, they make up about 1 percent of Colombia's population. Tribes live on communally owned land, which together covers about one-quarter

Population of Major Cities (2005)

City	Population
Bogotá	6,778,691
Medellín	2,223,660
Cali	2,075,380
Barranquilla	1,113,016
Cartagena	895,400

Afro-Colombians dance at a festival in Cartagena.

of the country. Many of Colombia's native peoples live in remote areas where they have little contact with outsiders. Because of their isolation, they maintained their traditional cultures.

As indigenous Colombians have more contact with other Colombians, their cultures change. Some now prefer Western clothing and buy goods such as bicycles, radios, and metal pots and pans. And many now send their children to the local schools to learn Spanish.

Caribbean Islanders

Both English and Dutch settlers lived on San Andrés and Providencia islands early in the 1600s. Later that century, the islands were used as a base by pirates who attacked Spanish ships. The pirate Henry Morgan is said to have hidden treasure on San Andrés. After the pirates left, a few English and Dutch settlers returned. But mostly, blacks from elsewhere in the Caribbean lived on the islands.

After Colombia became independent, it claimed the islands. Nicaragua, which is much closer to the islands, objected. The dispute was thought to have been settled in a 1928 treaty, but Nicaragua renounced the treaty in the 1980s, and arguments continue. For now, the islands remain Colombian.

English was long the dominant language on the islands. In recent decades, with the rise of regular air flights and easy shipping, the islands have been transformed. Thousands of Colombians from the mainland have settled in the islands. They now outnumber the black population. Slums are cropping up, violence and drug trafficking are increasing, and everywhere shops and hotels are being built. Spanish is now the islands' official language, and the most common religion is Roman Catholicism rather than Protestantism. Black families whose roots on the islands date back hundreds of years are struggling to retain their own traditions, language, and culture. The agricultural and fishing economy that long dominated San Andrés has given way to tourism, which employs more than half the population, few of them black.

Salt covers the dried, cracked surface of an evaporated lake on the Guajira Peninsula.

The Wayuu

The largest indigenous group in Colombia is the Wayuu, who are also known as the Guajiro. They number about 135,000 people.

The Wayuu live on the Guajira Peninsula, a hot, barren place that has long been a center of the drug trade. Although some Wayuu work as truck drivers or handle cargo, many still follow the traditional life of herding and farming. Their cattle and goats are their most prized possessions, and their wandering lifestyle is dictated by the animals' needs. The Wayuu try to collect as many animals as possible. Animals are treated so well that a traditional healer is called in when an animal is sick.

The peninsula is desperately short of water. Rain falls only between September and December, and then very lightly, so the Wayuu keep on the move to find water and grazing land. During the dry season, some Wayuu find work in the oil town of Maracaibo, Venezuela.

A Wayuu woman working at a salt mine has protected her face with a homemade sun cream.

Traditional Wayuu homes are built of mud, cane, and woven twigs plastered with clay and roofed with cactus. Today, an increasing number of Wayuu houses are built of cement and other modern building materials. Homes are usually divided into two rooms. The Wayuu hang hammocks for beds. Five or six houses make up a Wayuu settlement.

Wayuu men wear shirts and trousers. Women wear long, flowing, brightly colored robes called *mantas*. They cover their heads with cloth and paint their faces with a mixture of goat fat and charcoal. The women's clothing helps protect them from the hot sun. Women also wear a necklace called a *tuma*, which is made of semiprecious stones and is passed from mother to daughter.

About twenty-five thousand Arhuaco, Arsario, and Kogi live in the Sierra Nevada de Santa Marta. The snow-covered peaks that surround their villages are sacred to these tribes, who believe that the mountain range is the center of the universe. The arrival of colonists, developers, and drug traffickers drastically changed the lives of these deeply spiritual peoples. The Arhuaco, who have had most contact with other Colombians, have created an organization to defend their rights.

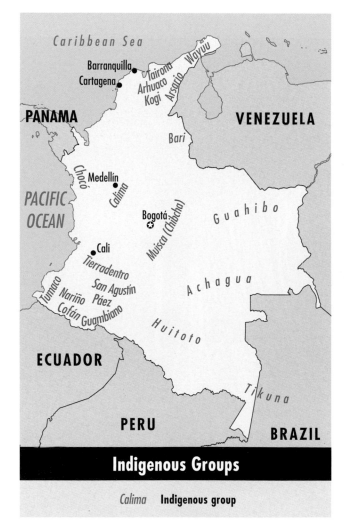

Indigenous Groups

Calima Indigenous group

When outsiders arrived, the Kogi moved deeper into the mountains. This enabled them to keep many age-old traditions. A typical Kogi village has a hut for men in the center, surrounded by smaller huts for women and children. Most huts are round with thatched, cone-shaped roofs. Priests, or *mamas*, are regarded as the most important members of the tribe. They decide all family and community matters and call all the people to the village when there are problems to be resolved.

Most Kogi farm the mountain slopes. Each family owns land at different levels. They grow potatoes,

An estimated six thousand Kogi live in the Sierra Nevada de Santa Marta. Tradition is strong among the Kogi.

manioc (also know as cassava), plantains, corn, and fruit. They also grow sugarcane, which they sell or exchange for useful items like knives or metal pots. They use the tough fiber of the agave plant to make hammocks, nets, bags, and rope. Kogi dress is a simple cotton tunic, usually knee-length. Men wear it over loosely woven pants. They also wear wide-brimmed hats. The mamas wear pointed hats.

The Guambiano live high in the Andes. They wear thick woolen clothes to stay warm.

The Páez and the Guambiano

The Páez and the Guambiano live in the southern Andean highlands. They grow crops on the slopes using simple wooden tools and ox-drawn plows. Families grow enough for themselves, with a little extra to sell in local markets. They keep some animals, including turkeys and sheep. The women also weave cotton and wool into garments and handicrafts that they sell locally.

Life can be hard in the cold mountain regions. To keep warm, people from these tribes often wrap themselves in large woolen *ruanas*, which are like ponchos but open down the front. The traditional dress of the Guambiano women is strikingly colorful. It consists of long, deep-blue skirts and ruanas, and many strings of white beads. Men wear a long skirt with a small poncho and a hat that is either round or flat.

Colombia's Cowboys

Spaniards first brought cattle to the Llanos. There, they met native people, had children together, and the *llanero* was born. The cowboys who fought alongside Simón Bolívar during the struggle for independence were llaneros.

Llaneros are skilled horsemen, adept at rounding up cattle. During the wet winters, they drive their cattle great distances to higher ground. And when dry summer returns, they make the long drive back. Llaneros sometimes demonstrate their skills in competitions in which they try to rope cows by grabbing their tails and dragging them to the ground.

Llaneros have unique music. Their main instruments are the harp, maracas, and a small guitar called a

cuatro. Their music has spread beyond their homeland. A llanero dance called the *joropo* has become the national dance of Venezuela.

Threatened Tribes

The Bari live in the Sierra de Perijá, in the northernmost part of the Cordillera Oriental. Oil was discovered on their land in the 1920s. This turned out to be devastating. Settlers and speculators drove the Bari from their homes. When the Bari resisted, many were killed. The remaining Bari moved higher into the mountains, but they still are not safe.

The discovery of oil also almost wiped out the Guahibo tribe, who live in the Llanos. For centuries, they had lived peacefully on the prairies. But when rumors of oil began, land investors moved in and tried to eject the Guahibo. The Indians fought back, sometimes violently. In response, the landowners called for help from the government and the army, and the Guahibo were overwhelmed.

Many different indigenous groups live in the rain forest. The main tribes of the Chocó are the Noanama, the Cuna, the Embera, and the Catio. Amazon tribes include the Tikuno, the Huitoto, and the Cofán. Most of these groups share a common problem: their land and way of life are threatened by people who cut the forest for timber or clear the land for farming and ranching.

Indigenous peoples of the Chocó and the Amazon share a similar way of life. The forest provides many of their needs. They make wood and thatch homes, hunt animals, and use plants to treat the sick. In cleared areas, they grow plantains,

The Emera hunt using blowguns. A dart tipped with poison is put in one end and blown out the other.

peanuts, and cotton. Canoes made from hollowed-out tree trunks are their main form of transportation. Men catch fish in the rivers using nets, basket traps, spears, and lines.

The forest people believe that their shamans, or priests, can help them contact the spirit world. They also believe that their gods are related to the natural world around them. During rituals, they paint their bodies, dance, and play music on reed or bamboo flutes and drums.

Colombia's Languages

Spanish is spoken throughout Colombia, but many indigenous languages have survived. About seventy-eight languages are still in use in Colombia. Most of these belong to the Arawak, Carib, and Guarani language groups.

Colombians claim to speak the purest form of Spanish in Latin America. The main variation is on the Caribbean coast, where people speak more quickly and with a regional accent.

A man in the Chocó collects curare. Curare is a poison that some native Colombians use when hunting.

Odd Colombian Expressions

A *lagarto* ("lizard") is a person who wants to become high class by meeting important people but who makes those people uncomfortable.

A *sardina* or a *sardino* (a "sardine"—a fish) is a teenage girl or boy.

A *voltiarepas* is a person who is always changing sides. It comes from two words: *voltear*, which means "to turn over," and *arepas*, a corn griddle pancake popular in Colombia.

¡Es un verraco! means "He's great!" or "He's very courageous!" *Verraco* means "pig" or "boar." The expression was once an insult.

Many Names

Colombians use two last names. The first last name is the father's last name, and the second last name is the mother's.

Children are often given two or three first names. People in the Medellín region like to call children by the English version of a name. For example, John is popular. It is often used with another name such as Jairo, so John Jairo is typical.

Names that include María are also common. These include AnaMaría, María de la Paz, María del Carmen, María Luisa, and María José. For boys, many "double" names include Juan or José, for example, Juan Pablo, Juan Carlos, and José María. Many names honor important religious figures, like José (Saint Joseph), María (the Virgin Mary), Juan (Saint John), and Jesus. The combination JuanMaría is used for boys.

Nicknames are popular in Colombia. Some common names have standard nicknames. For example, people named José are called Pepe. Francisco becomes Pancho, Jesus is Chucho, and Luis is Lucho.

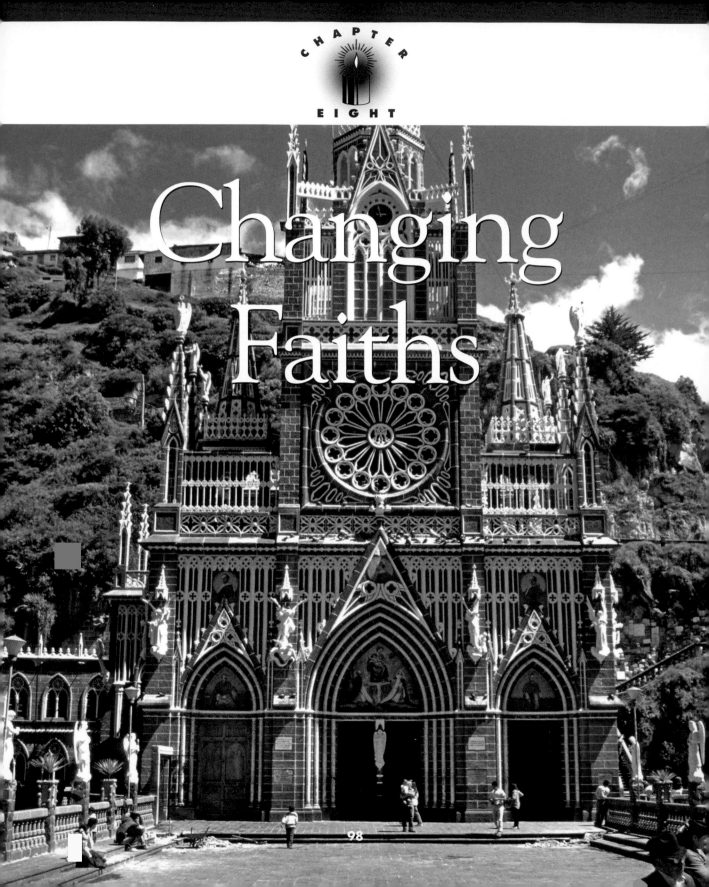

Changing
Faiths

A religious procession makes its way through the town of Tunja during Easter week.

Most of Colombia's national holidays are religious, including Christmas, Easter, and Corpus Christi. The Easter celebrations in the beautiful colonial city of Popayán attract visitors from all over Colombia and neighboring countries. Statues of all the city's saints are paraded through the streets in elaborate processions.

Many villages and towns in Colombia also celebrate their special saint's day. On these days, the towns break out with parades, processions, bell-ringing, music, and dancing.

Opposite: **The Sanctuary of Our Lady of Las Lajas is built into the side of a canyon in southern Colombia.**

Pope Paul VI celebrates Mass in front of gigantic crowds in Bogotá in 1968.

The Catholic Church

In 1968, Pope Paul VI, the head of the Catholic Church, visited Colombia. Never before had a pope visited Latin America, a land where the Catholic religion had been dominant since the arrival of the Spanish four centuries earlier. In Colombia, every city, town, and even small village has a church.

Colombia celebrated the pope's visit with special events. Huge crowds gathered in the main square in front of Bogotá's cathedral for a blessing. A special temple was built for other ceremonies, and some of the faithful traveled the last few miles on their knees. The pope, however, had arrived at a time when the mood of the Colombian people was changing.

After Colombia became independent from Spain, the Catholic Church was powerful in

Religious Holidays

Epiphany	January 6
St. Joseph's Day	March 19
Holy Thursday	March or April
Good Friday	March or April
Easter	March or April
Corpus Christi	June
Saints Peter and Paul Day	June 29
Assumption Day	August 15
All Saints' Day	November 1
Immaculate Conception Day	December 8
Christmas	December 25

Our Lady of Las Lajas

The Sanctuary of Our Lady of Las Lajas is a massive church built on a bridge over a deep river gorge near Colombia's border with Ecuador. According to legend, in the eighteenth century, an image of the Virgin Mary, the mother of Jesus, appeared on the steep rocks above the bridge. The church was built in 1803 to commemorate this event. It was rebuilt about a hundred years later in a spectacular design that incorporates the rock that holds the image as part of the high altar.

Many pilgrims visit Las Lajas. Some of them leave notes thanking the Virgin Mary for miracles they believe have occurred.

The Salt Cathedral

A huge mountain with a core of salt stands next to the town of Zipaquirá, about 30 miles (50 km) north of Bogotá. This area has Colombia's richest salt mines. People have been mining the salt here since the time of the Muisca.

Deep underground, miners carved an amazing cathedral out of the salt. It replaced an earlier structure. The new cathedral, which opened in 1995, can hold at least ten thousand people. The altar is a solid block of salt said to weigh 18 tons.

the young country. It often sided with Conservatives and large landowners. At that time, the church opposed other religions, which were seen as a threat to its status and power. Late in the nineteenth century, Liberals tried to reduce the power of the church by taking away church lands and allowing people to choose their religion. But when Conservatives returned to power, they overturned these reforms.

By the mid-twentieth century, some church leaders were recommending changes to help the growing number of poor and poorly educated Colombians. One priest, Camilo Torres, even left the church and became a rebel speaker and later a fighter. He was killed in combat by the army in 1966.

After the pope's visit in 1968, some fundamental changes took place. In 1973, the church gave up some of its control over education. In 1976, it agreed to allow marriages to end in certain cases. It was not until 1991, however, that Colombia allowed divorce for all marriages, whether civil or religious.

Moving to Other Faiths

In the mid-1980s, some 97.5 percent of Colombians, whether black, mulatto, mestizo, or indigenous, called themselves Catholic. Most non-Catholics were black Protestants who lived on Colombia's Caribbean islands. In recent years, however, millions of Colombians have moved to other faiths. Today, only about 81 percent of Colombians are Catholic.

Evangelical Protestant groups work in many South American countries, including Colombia. The evangelicals teach a strict interpretation of the Bible. They have been

Colombia's Religions

Roman Catholicism	81%
Non-evangelical Protestantism	10%
Evangelical Protestantism	3.5%
No religious belief	1.9%
Other	3.6%

A Mormon church in Colombia. Mormonism is among the fastest-growing religions in the nation.

particularly successful among Colombia's poor. Jehovah's Witnesses, Mormons, and Lutherans are among the rising religious groups in Colombia. Today, the nation is home to an estimated 180,000 Seventh-Day Adventists, 130,000 Mormons, and 120,000 Jehovah's Witnesses.

There are also 5,000 to 10,000 Jews in Colombia. The country has small numbers of Muslims, Buddhists, Hindus, and Baha'is, too.

Indigenous Beliefs

The traditional beliefs of Colombia's indigenous peoples are often connected to nature. The Kogi, for example, see the universe as an egg-shaped space. The four main directions are occupied by the mythical ancestors of the Kogi. In the north are the opossum and the armadillo; in the south, the puma and the deer; in the east, the jaguar and the peccary; and in the west, the eagle and the snake.

The Noanama Hai

When they are young, Noanama children of the Chocó are given a small wooden figure as a toy. This figure represents their spiritual guide, or *hai*. Parents make sure the children take care of the hai, because it must never be lost. The Noanama always carry their hai with them, even when they are adults, believing it will protect them from evil and from the vengeful spirits of wild animals.

The Kogi's cosmic space is divided into nine layers. The nine layers are the nine daughters of the mother goddess who created the universe. Each represents a certain kind of earth, from barren sand to rich soil. We live in the world of the fifth daughter, who represents fertile black soil.

The main task of the *mamas*, or priests, is to carry out rituals to keep order in the universe. The Kogi believe that mamas are responsible for the rising and setting of the Sun, for the seasons, and for ensuring that the world and its people are fertile. They also heal the sick.

When Kogi men gather in their village hut, mamas lead the meetings, which can last for two or three days. Mamas also lead meetings high in the mountains. They make offerings of stones, seeds, shells, or pieces of thread, cotton, or hair. Sometimes, their rituals include masked dancers and the music of flutes, rattles, and small drums.

A Kogi mama in the Sierra Nevada de Santa Marta. Mamas are chosen when they are born and are in training for about eighteen years.

Changing Faiths   **105**

CHAPTER

NINE

Culture
and Sports

THE EARLY CIVILIZATIONS IN COLOMBIA LEFT A RICH cultural heritage. Skilled craftspeople transformed clay into statues and pots. They decorated the pots with drawings of animals and birds. Zigzag designs using a variety of dots and whorls were also favorites. Early Colombians made music on panpipes, some made of reeds and others of gold.

Opposite: **The Spanish tradition of bullfighting is popular in Colombia.**

This Quimbaya statue dates back to before Europeans arrived in South America.

Many modern Colombians look to these traditions for inspiration. Jewelers today make gold objects using ancient methods. The folk artists of Pasto use a traditional natural varnish to create patterns on wooden vases, plates, stools, and tabletops.

Colombia's most famous artist today is Fernando Botero. He was born in 1932 to a humble family in Medellín. In 1951, he moved to Bogotá, and he later studied in Europe and New York. Botero's paintings and sculptures are famous for their distinctive round figures. He depicts both people and animals using round, exaggerated shapes.

The Presidential Family, by Fernando Botero. Botero is famous for his round, sometimes mocking figures.

The Gold Museum

Colombia's ancient goldsmiths created exquisite objects of thinly beaten gold. The images they made leave no doubt that the spirits were considered all-powerful. The El Dorado ceremony involved hundreds of golden objects. Many rulers were buried with gold masks and other finery.

Colombia's ancient artistic heritage is on glorious display in the Gold Museum in Bogotá. The museum tells the story of the region's early peoples, showing their crafts and ways of life. The museum is filled with case after case of gold masks, breastplates, animal figures, ornaments, and drinking vessels.

A cumbia band performs in Cartagena. Cumbia got its start in the area around Cartagena and is now popular throughout Central and South America.

Perhaps the most popular Colombian music is the Afro-Colombian *cumbia* from the Atlantic coast. The traditional cumbia groups are the *conjunto de cumbia* (which usually consists of four percussion instruments and a *caño de millo*, a type of clarinet) and the *conjunto de gaitas* (which uses two flutes, percussion, and maracas). Maracas are gourds containing a handful of small pebbles that make a sharp, rattling sound when shaken. The *gaita* flutes have origins in the music of native peoples of the Sierra Nevada de Santa Marta.

Vallenatos are like folk stories set to music. According to legend, vallenato music began with a man named Francisco el Hombre. In the days when there was no telephone or newspapers or mail, news was sent from one village to another in the Magdalena River valley by a sort of town crier. The legend says that Francisco el Hombre added an accordion and "sang" the news from town to town.

Traditionally, *vallenato* lyrics tell love stories and dramatic tales. Vallenato is accompanied by small drums and a *guacharaca*, a wooden tube that is scratched with a small metallic fork. Pop musician Carlos Vives has fused vallenato with rock, pop, and Caribbean rhythms to great success.

Carlos Vives is both a popular musician and a successful actor.

The *bambuco* is Colombia's national dance. It is usually accompanied by stringed instruments including the *tiple*, a small twelve-stringed guitar.

The South American music with the most African influences comes from Colombia's Pacific coast. Typical

Shakira

Shakira Isabel Mebarak Ripoll, known to her fans as simply Shakira, is a Colombian singer and songwriter. She has sold fifty million albums, making her the best-selling Colombian artist of all time. Shakira's music has earned her a Grammy Award and many Latin Grammys.

Shakira was born in 1977 to parents of Spanish and Lebanese descent. Growing up in Barranquilla, she began writing and composing music at age eight but was apparently rejected by her school choir because her voice was too strong!

Her early albums, which were released in the 1990s, include *Pies Descalzos* ("Bare Feet") and *Dónde Están Los Ladrones?* ("Where Are the Thieves?"). In 2001, she released her first English-language album, *Laundry Service*, which sold fifteen million copies worldwide. In 2006, her song "Hips Don't Lie" became the number-one single in the United States, the United Kingdom, and elsewhere around the world.

In 2001, Shakira founded a charity that helps protect children from the violence in Colombia. The charity builds special schools where displaced children can be fed and educated.

Colombia's Greatest Writer

Gabriel García Márquez is one of the great figures of modern literature, and many consider him the most important Latin American novelist of all time. He was awarded the highest honor in literature, the Nobel Prize, in 1982.

García Márquez was born in Aracataca on March 6, 1927. Aracataca is a small town in the "banana belt," close to the Sierra Nevada de Santa Marta. Stories of the great massacre of banana workers in March 1928 in nearby Cienaga were still fresh as he grew up. Some of his own background and an account of the massacre are threaded into his classic work *One Hundred Years of Solitude*.

Another of his well-known novels, *Love in the Time of Cholera*, is based on a family courtship. His other works include *The General in His Labyrinth*, based on the life of liberator Simón Bolívar; *Love and Other Demons*, set in eighteenth-century Cartagena; and *News of a Kidnapping*, about drugs and kidnapping.

instruments are the marimba, which is similar to a xylophone, and the *guasá*, a rattle containing seeds. The musicians also play many different types of drums.

Colombian music often includes African-style drums. Accordions are also common.

Colombia's national soccer team poses in 1993. Wild celebrations erupted when the team defeated Argentina.

Colombians are passionate about soccer. When a favored team wins, the streets are filled with a parade of cars and the constant honking of horns.

One of Colombia's greatest victories came in 1993, when Colombia beat Argentina 5–0. Before the game, the Argentine superstar Maradona had boasted that he was certain Argentina would beat Colombia easily. This made Argentina's defeat even more embarrassing. Colombia's victory was celebrated like a national holiday, with parties in most every house in Colombia.

Colombians faced bitter disappointment the following year when the United States defeated Colombia 2–1 in the first round of the World Cup, soccer's most important tournament. This shocked many people, because Colombia was one of the favorites to win the cup. The defeat was even more humiliating because the deciding goal was scored accidentally by the Colombian defender Andrés Escobar. This error almost certainly cost Escobar his life. He was killed a few days later in a bar in Medellín.

Bullfighting was introduced by the Spanish in the colonial era, and it remains popular with many Colombians. Many cities have bullrings that can seat thousands.

Cycling Heroes

Martin Emilio "Cochise" Rodríguez is a former world champion cyclist and a national hero. He was born in 1942 into a poor family. He made it to the top by sheer effort and courage.

Luis Alberto "Lucho" Herrera (left), another great Colombian cyclist, was born in 1961. He got the nickname El Jardinerito ("The Little Gardener") because he worked as a gardener. Riding his heavy gardener's bicycle up and down the steep mountain roads gave him strength and endurance. Herrera won in mountain cycling in the Tour de France, the Tour d'Espagne, and the Tour d'Italie. He was kidnapped and held for twenty-four hours by the rebel group FARC in 2000, before being released.

Everyday Life

A brightly painted bus livens the streets of Jardín in northwestern Colombia.

COLOMBIA'S CITIES ARE MUCH LIKE CITIES ANYWHERE. The streets are bustling with businesspeople and lined with fashionable shops. Long lines of traffic create ever more pollution.

City Life

Middle- and working-class Colombians live much like people in North America. They dress in business suits, or jeans and shirts. Many work as lawyers, teachers, doctors, and businesspeople. Others work in shops and factories. The less skilled find work as taxi drivers, secretaries, bank tellers, or domestic servants. Some sell trinkets, cigarettes, candy, and other items from street stalls.

Opposite: **A woman at a beauty pageant in Pasto**

A Different Kind of Mayor

Antanas Mockus was elected mayor of Bogotá in 1993 and again in 2001. He is a colorful politician. On one occasion, he himself took a shower in a commercial about conserving water. He also introduced a "Night for Women," when men were asked to stay at home and look after the children so that women could enjoy a safe night out under the protective eye of the city's female police officers.

Mockus was born in 1952, the son of Lithuanian immigrants. He became a mathematician and then principal of the Colombian National University. He left that post to become mayor. During his time in office, he oversaw many city improvements. Drinking water was provided to all homes. Traffic accidents dropped by more than 50 percent, and the murder rate plunged by 70 percent. Seven thousand community security groups were formed, making Bogotá a much safer place. Not every effort was a success, however. He was unable to reduce poverty and unemployment in the city.

Although a popular mayor, Mockus had little following in the countryside, and his two bids for the presidency, in 1998 and 2006, failed.

Street Children

An estimated five thousand homeless children sleep on the streets of Bogotá. They survive by begging, running errands, washing cars, cleaning shoes, or anything else they can think of. Many become involved in drugs and crime. Occasionally, the authorities have a "clean-up" and remove the children from the streets, but it isn't long before they return.

Most middle-class and working-class Colombians live in modern apartment buildings. The poor live in slums on the outskirts of cities. Their homes often lack electricity or running water. The contrast between their rundown shacks and the rich suburbs is striking. A few very wealthy people live in luxurious houses protected by guards, dogs, and barbed-wire fences. They have many servants and large grounds.

Bogotá's Ciudad Bolívar is the largest slum in Colombia. It is home to more than seven hundred thousand people.

Rural Life

Many people who live along the coasts or in the Amazon lowlands work as fishermen, farmers, lumbermen, or dockworkers. A few are miners. Life is casual in the hot, wet climate. People wear T-shirts and shorts or jeans. Things are not so different on the sugarcane plantations in the river valleys, where the climate is similar.

But the Andes are another world. Life is difficult high in the cordilleras. A farmer often toils from dawn until dusk on his small plot of land, using only an ox-drawn plow and wooden tools. The people of the Andes have few luxuries. Local celebrations are their main relaxation.

Many Colombians make their living fishing. Here, oyster fishermen unload their boats near Santa Marta.

Elsewhere on the mountain slopes, coffee workers have a more comfortable lifestyle. The National Federation of Coffee Growers has helped them get electricity, running water, hospitals, schools, and some good roads.

Parades take over the streets of Barranquilla during Carnival, a wild four-day event.

Festivals

Colombia has a festival for every day of the year. Among the most famous are the Cali Fair, the Barranquilla Carnival, the Iberoamerican Theater Festival, and the Flower Festival in Medellín.

Carnival is one of Colombia's biggest festivals. It is a time for fun and eating before the solemn

National Holidays in Colombia

New Year's Day	January 1
Labor Day	May 1
Independence Day	July 20
Battle of Boyacá	August 7
Columbus Day	October 12
Independence of Cartagena	November 11

Dancers perform at a parade in Barranquilla. Many Colombian towns have Carnival celebrations, but none can match Barranquilla's.

time called Lent (the 40 days before Easter). In Barranquilla, Carnival is an exuberant mix of rhythm and color. The streets are filled with music and parades. Parties with nonstop music and masked dancers last for days.

Another well-known festival is Pasto's Festival of Blacks and Whites. January 5 is the *Día de los Negros* ("Day of the Black Ones"), and January 6 is the *Día de los Blancos* ("Day of the White Ones"). The festival dates back to the time when January 5 was a day of celebration for slaves. Their masters showed approval by painting their faces black. The next day, the slaves painted their faces white. Today, the boys of Pasto chase the girls, dabbing their faces with black shoe polish.

Education

In Colombia, all children aged six to twelve are expected to attend primary school. They go for six or seven years before moving to secondary school. After secondary school, students can continue on to college. Colombia has many universities and institutions of higher education.

Public schools are free in Colombia. Some parents instead send their children to private or church-run schools. The school year runs from February to November in Bogotá, while in many other places it runs from August to June. The best schools are in urban areas, where there are enough teachers, classrooms, books, and equipment. But even in cities, some schools have to run in shifts, with the younger children attending in the mornings and the older students in the afternoons or evenings.

In primary schools in Colombia, there are an average of twenty-six students for every teacher.

Hitting the Frog

A popular game in Colombia uses a wooden box called a *rana* ("frog"). Slots in the top of the box are marked by numbers from 100 to 500. At the back is a brass frog worth 1,000. Players get five brass rings to throw at the slots and the frog. The player who scores the most points wins.

Some children in rural areas do not go to school because their parents need them to help work the land. In remote areas of the Amazon, the Chocó, and the Llanos, children may face difficulties in school because Spanish is not their first language.

Educators have sometimes tried to reach children in remote areas through radio or television. Regular educational broadcasts are also aimed at adults who have had no schooling. Fifty years ago in Colombia, almost half the people over ten years of age could not read or write. Today, 93 percent of Colombians are literate.

Staying in Touch

Today, almost everyone in Colombia has access to radio, and television reaches about 90 percent of the population. Computers and the Internet are playing an increasing role in Colombia's way of life, and cybercafes are everywhere.

Several of Colombia's leading national papers are associated with political parties. *El Espectador* and *El Tiempo* are Liberal, while *La República* and *El Siglo* are Conservative. Most cities and towns publish their own newspapers and magazines, but it is now possible to buy a Bogotá newspaper in remote cities on the day it is published.

Women making empanadas. These pastries, usually filled with meat, can be either baked or fried.

Good to Eat

Tasty snacks like *chorizos*, *empanadas*, *arepas*, and *pasteles de yuca* can be found all over Colombia. Chorizos are sausages that are usually well seasoned but not spicy. Empanadas are pastries filled with meat, chicken, vegetables, or olives, and arepas are corn griddle pancakes. *Pasteles de yuca* are pastries made from the flour of a wild tuber called yuca. They are filled with rice, meat, and peas. *Buñuelos*, a sort of doughnut made of corn flour and cheese, are also popular. Fruit stands sell *salpición*, a mixture of finely chopped fruits in orange juice.

An Ordinary Lunch

Perhaps the dish that comes closest to a Colombian national dish is the *almuerzo corriente*, or *bandeja*. It is a typical lunch. The meal begins with a hearty soup. It is followed by rice, potatoes or fried plantains, a salad, a fried egg, meat, and beans or lentils. Fresh fruit juice is often included.

Regional dishes include *ajiaco de pollo* from Bogotá. This soup includes chicken, corn, and potatoes and is served with cream, capers, and chunks of avocado. Cali's traditional dish is *sancocho de gallina*, a soup composed mostly of chicken, plantains, corn, cilantro, yuca root, and other seasonings. Soups are common in the highlands. For breakfast, the main dish is often *changua*, a meat broth with potatoes and freshly chopped cilantro and scallions. *Sopa de pan* is a main-course soup that includes bread, eggs, and cheese.

Fish is the basic food of the Amazon and Chocó regions. On the Caribbean coast, coconut rice with spicy fish and lobster is popular. In the Tolima region, *tamales* are a delicacy. Tamales are made of a cornmeal dough filled with peas, carrots, potatoes, rice, chicken, pork, and various spices. They are wrapped in plantain leaves and boiled for three to four hours.

Coffee is served with every meal and at many other times during the day. A small cup of coffee with lots of sugar, known as *tinto*, is a great favorite.

The Best of Colombia

Colombia is a country both blessed and cursed. Violence and terrorism have tormented the nation for decades. Yet Colombia is also rich and welcoming in many ways. It is rich in natural resources and energy, and its economy is strong. Its wealth of wildlife and natural habitats far exceeds that of most other countries. It is graced with stunning landscapes, from snowcapped volcanoes to white-sand beaches. And perhaps most of all, Colombia is rich in the warmth of its people and culture.

Brightly painted houses dot the lush landscape on Providencia Island.

Timeline

Colombian History

Indigenous peoples make pottery near what is now Cartagena.	ca. 3000 B.C.

World History

2500 B.C.	Egyptians build the pyramids and the Sphinx in Giza.
563 B.C.	The Buddha is born in India.
A.D. 313	The Roman emperor Constantine legalizes Christianity.
610	The Prophet Muhammad begins preaching a new religion called Islam.
1054	The Eastern (Orthodox) and Western (Roman Catholic) Churches break apart.
1095	The Crusades begin.
1215	King John seals the Magna Carta.
1300s	The Renaissance begins in Italy.
1347	The plague sweeps through Europe.
1453	Ottoman Turks capture Constantinople, conquering the Byzantine Empire.
1492	Columbus arrives in North America.
1500s	Reformers break away from the Catholic Church, and Protestantism is born.

Colombian History (continued)

Spanish explorers sail along Colombia's Caribbean coast.	A.D. 1500
Spaniards found Santa Marta, their first permanent settlement in South America.	1525
Gonzalo Jiménez de Quesada founds Santa Fe de Bogotá.	1538
The Spanish government creates the Audiencia of Santa Fe de Bogotá.	1549
Sir Francis Drake destroys much of Cartagena.	1586
Spain creates the Viceroyalty of New Granada, with Santa Fe de Bogotá as the capital.	1717

1776	The U.S. Declaration of Independence is signed.

Colombian History

A rebellion begins in New Granada.	1781
Colombia wins its independence.	1819
The nation of Gran Colombia is created.	1821
Gran Colombia breaks apart; Colombia becomes the Republic of New Granada.	1830
The Republic of New Granada is renamed Colombia.	1863
The War of a Thousand Days causes almost 100,000 deaths.	1899–1902
Panama gains its independence from Colombia.	1903
About 200,000 people die in a civil war called *La Violencia*.	ca. 1948–1962
The Liberals and the Conservatives agree to govern together in the National Front.	1958
Ciudad Perdida is discovered.	1972
The National Front ends.	1974
Gabriel García Márquez wins the Nobel Prize for Literature.	1982
Nevado del Ruiz erupts, killing 25,000 people.	1985
A new constitution is written.	1991
Álvaro Uribe Vélez is elected president.	2002

World History

1789	The French Revolution begins.
1865	The American Civil War ends.
1879	The first practical light bulb is invented.
1914	World War I begins.
1917	The Bolshevik Revolution brings communism to Russia.
1929	A worldwide economic depression begins.
1939	World War II begins.
1945	World War II ends.
1957	The Vietnam War begins.
1969	Humans land on the Moon.
1975	The Vietnam War ends.
1989	The Berlin Wall is torn down as communism crumbles in Eastern Europe.
1991	The Soviet Union breaks into separate states.
2001	Terrorists attack the World Trade Center in New York City and the Pentagon in Washington, D.C.

Fast Facts

Official name: Republic of Colombia

Capital: Bogotá

Official language: Spanish

Bogotá

Colombia's flag

Providencia Island

Official religion:	None
Year of founding:	1819
Founder:	Simón Bolívar
National anthem:	"Himno Nacional de la República de Colombia" ("National Anthem of the Republic of Colombia")
Government:	Multiparty republic
Chief of state:	President
Area:	439,735 square miles (1,138,908 sq km)
Latitude and longitude of geographic center:	3°45' N, 73° W
Borders:	The Caribbean Sea to the north, Venezuela and Brazil to the east, Peru and Ecuador to the south, the Pacific Ocean to the west, and Panama to the northwest
Highest elevation:	Pico Cristóbal Colón, 19,020 feet (5,797 m)
Lowest elevation:	Sea level, along the coasts
Lowest average temperature:	46°F (8°C) in January in Bogotá
Highest average temperature:	92°F (33°C) in July in Cali
Annual average rainfall:	100 inches (254 cm) in the rain forest; 30 inches (76 cm) along the Caribbean Sea
National population (2006 est.):	43,593,035

Our Lady of Las Lajas

Population of largest cities (2005):		
	Bogotá	6,778,691
	Medellín	2,223,660
	Cali	2,075,380
	Barranquilla	1,113,016
	Cartagena	895,400

Famous landmarks:
- ▶ *San Agustín,* Popayán
- ▶ *Tierradentro,* Popayán
- ▶ *Fort of San Felipe,* Cartagena
- ▶ *Salt Cathedral,* Zipaquirá
- ▶ *Sanctuary of Our Lady of Las Lajas,* Ipiales
- ▶ *Gold Museum,* Bogotá
- ▶ *Puracé National Park,* Popayán

Industry: Mining and manufacturing are both important in Colombia. About 60 percent of the world's emeralds come from Colombia. Nickel and gold are also mined there. Coal and oil are major Colombian exports. Colombia's major manufactured goods include processed foods and beverages, textiles and clothing, machinery, paper and paper products, and transportation equipment.

Currency: The Colombian peso is the basic monetary unit. In 2007, US$1 equaled 2,235 pesos.

Weights and measures: Colombians use both the metric system and traditional Spanish weights and measures.

Literacy: 93%

Currency

Schoolchildren

Gabriel García Márquez

Common Spanish words and phrases:

Adíos	Goodbye
Buenos días	Good morning
Buenas noches	Good evening/ good night
Cuanto?	How much?
Cuantos?	How many?
Dónde está …?	Where is …?
Gracias	Thank you
Por favor	Please

Famous Colombians:

Fernando Botero (1932–)
Artist

Blas de Lezo (1688–1741)
Defender of Cartagena

Gabriel García Márquez (1927–)
Writer and Nobel Prize winner

Luis Alberto "Lucho" Herrara (1961–)
Cyclist

Carlos Lleras Restrepo (1908–1994)
Politician and historian

Antonio Nariño (1765–1823)
Independence leader

Rafael Nuñez (1825–1894)
Politician

Martin Emilio "Cochise" Rodríguez (1942–)
Cyclist

Francisco de Paula Santander (1792–1840)
General and politician

Shakira (1977–)
(Shakira Isabel Mebarak Ripoll)
Singer-songwriter

To Find Out More

Books

▶ Borass, Tracey. *Colombia*. Mankato, MN: Bridgestone Books, 2002.

▶ DuBois, Jill. *Colombia*. New York: Marshall Cavendish, 2002.

▶ Lim, Bee Hong. *Welcome to Colombia*. Milwaukee: Gareth Stevens Publishing, 2000.

▶ Lopata, Peg. *Colombia*. San Diego: Lucent Books, 2004.

▶ *Nations in Conflict: Colombia*. Chicago: Blackbirch Press, 2005.

Web Sites

▶ **The Gold Museum**
http://www.banrep.org/museo/eng/home.htm
To read all about the museum.

▶ **National Geographic Society**
http://www3.nationalgeographic.
com/places/countries/country_
colombia.html
*For an overview of Colombia, complete
with photos, maps, videos, and music.*

▶ **The World Factbook**
https://www.cia.gov/cia/publications/
factbook/geos/co.html
*For an excellent overview of the
geography, government, and economy
of Colombia.*

Organizations and Embassies

▶ **Embassy of Colombia**
2118 Leroy Place N.W.
Washington, D.C. 20008
(202) 387-8338

Index

Page numbers in *italics*
indicate illustrations.

blacks, 85, 86, 87, 88
Calima, 44
Catio, 95
children, 91, *92*, *93*, 105, 118, *118*, 122–124, *123*
clothing, 45, *92*, *93*, *93*, 117, 120
Cofán, 95
cowboys, *76*, 94, *94*
criollos, 49, 51
Cuna, 95
education, 122–124, *123*
Embera, 95
Emera, *95*
employment, 72, 117, 120, 121
expressions for, 97
foods, 125–126, *125*, *126*
Guahibo, 94
Guambiano, 93, *93*
homelessness, 118, *118*
housing, *24*, 44, 90, 95, 119, *119*, *127*
Huitoto, 95
immigrants, 86
indigenous, 86, 87–88, 89, 95–96, 104
Kogi, 10, 91–92, *92*, 104–105, *105*
literacy rate, 124
mestizos, 85, 86, *86*
Muisca, 15, 44, *44*, 46, 47, 48, 68
mulattos, 85, 86, 87
names, 97
nicknames, 97
Noanama, 95, 105
Páez, 93
peninsulares, 49, 51
population, 27, 69, 85, 87
poverty, 72, 87, 118
prehistoric, 43–44
Quimbaya, 44, 45
Sinú, 44, 45

slavery, 48, 49, 50, 54, 87, 122
Tairona, 10, 44
Tikuno, 95
Tolima, 44
Tumaco, 44
Wayuu, *84*, 89–90, *90*
whites, 85, 86
women, 90, 91, *93*, 118
zambos, 86
Zaque, 47
Zipa, 47
Peru, 11, 12, 17, 24, 25, 46, 47, 48, 53
pesos (currency), 77, *77*
Pico Cristóbal Colón, 18, 22
Pies Descalzos (Shakira), 112
pirates, 49, 88
Plan Colombia, 60–61
plant life, 11, *12*, 14, 15, 25, *25*, 26, *26*, 31, 32, 33, 34, *34*, 35, 36, 40, 61, *70*, 73, 92
Plaza Bolívar, 50
Plaza de los Coches ("Square of the Carriages"), 50
Pointis, Baron de, 49
poison dart frogs, 41, *41*
Popayán, 20, *20*, 45, 48, 99
population, 27, 69, 85, 87
prehistoric people, 43–44
Presidential Family (Fernando Botero), *108*
Protestants, 63, 88, 103–104
Providencia Island, *16*, 29, *29*, 88, *127*
Pumarejo, Alfonso López, 56
Puracé National Park, 32
Puracé Volcano, 20
Putumayo River, 24, 25

Meet the Author

"COLOMBIA WAS MY FIRST STOPOVER ON A LONG FLIGHT to South America," says Marion Morrison. She was on her way from her home in London, England, to a job in Bolivia. "I'll never forget the tropical atmosphere and the welcoming words of Spanish." Since then, she has returned to Colombia many times. She has enjoyed driving along the Andes, living in Bogotá, and exploring the Sierra Nevada de Santa Marta.

Marion has spent years in Latin America, and she is often asked which country is her favorite. She says, "I feel it's unfair to make quick comparisons as each has so much to offer, but one Colombian city stands out among dozens I have visited. Cartagena, on the Caribbean coast, has an enormously rich history, and pirates and adventurers are just a part." Marion studied history at the University of Wales, and her mind turns naturally to a country's foundations. She visited Cartagena in Spain to find out more about the history of Colombia. "When I got back to the old streets of Colombia's Cartagena and deep inside the enormous Spanish fortresses, times past came alive with romance and, all too frequently, deep sadness."

Marion has written many books for the Enchantment of the World series. To keep up with what's going on in South America, she travels frequently and stays in touch with her friends across the continent by e-mail and telephone. Many of her travels have been with her husband, Tony, who has written books and made television films set in South America. Together, they founded a picture library based on their work.

Photo Credits

Photographs © 2008:

age fotostock: 62 (Juan Antonio Alonso), 28 (Fabio Braibanti/Marka), 55 (Andoni Canela), 70 (Toño Labra), 57 (Tramonto)

Alamy Images: 26 (mediacolor's), 50 (Doug Moler/Danita Delimont), 105 (Brian Moser/Eye Obiquitous), 99, 123, 133 top (Roberto Orrú), 32 (Edward Parker), 110, 113 bottom (James Quine), 98 (Pep Roig), 10 (David South), 126 (TNT Magazine), 27 bottom (Peter M. Wilson)

AP Images: 14 (Luis Benavides), 80 (Miguel Garcia/El Espectador), 15 (Gold Museum), 111 (Branimir Kvartuc), 12 (Julian Lineros), 118 bottom (William Fernando Martinez), 109 (Museo del Oro), 31, 121 (Fernando Vergara)

Art Directors and TRIP/Jorge Monaco: 127

Art Resource, NY/Digital Image/The Museum of Modern Art/SCALA: 108

Bridgeman Art Library International Ltd., London/New York/Private Collection: 51

Carlos Sastoque: 22, 35, 77 top, 104, 132 bottom

Corbis Images: 56, 66 top (Bettmann), cover, back cover, 6 (Jan Butchofsky-Houser), 113 top, 133 bottom (Bernardo De Niz/Reuters), 88 (Macduff Everton), 61 (Jose Miguel Gomez/Reuters), 2, 20, 84, 116, 125 (Jeremy Horner), 8 (Dave G. Houser), 25 (Hulton-Deutsch Collection), 21 (Jacques Langevin/Sygma), 11 (Albeiro Lopera/Reuters), 59 (Alain Masiero/Sygma), 86 (Carl & Ann Purcell), 72 (Enzo & Paolo Ragazzini), 112 (Mike Segar/Reuters), 23 (Ted Spiegel), 60 (Ray Stubblebine/Reuters), 40 (Terry Whittaker/Frank Lane Picture Agency)

Danita Delimont Stock Photography/Doug Moler: 87

Getty Images: 63, 118 top (Rodrigo Arangua/AFP), 114 (Shaun Botterill), 115 (Mondelo/AFP)

Kevin Schafer: 30, 38

Lonely Planet Images/Krzysztof Dydynski: 17, 29, 37, 42, 79, 101, 117, 132 top

Minden Pictures: 33 (Tui de Roy), 41 top, 95, 96 (Mark Moffett)

NHPA/Mark Bowler: 39 bottom

Photo Researchers, NY: 36 (John S. Dunning), 41 bottom (Claudine Laabs), 39 top (Kjell B. Sandved)

Reuters: 106 (Carlos Duran), 71, 90, 122 (Jose Miguel Gomez), 83

ShutterStock, Inc.: 64, 131 top (Arteki), 68, 130 left (Andrey Shchekalev)

South American Pictures: 81, 89 (Nicholas Bright), 92 (Britt Dyer), 9, 45, 74, 78 (Mike Harding), 65, 66 bottom, 94, 102, 119 (Jason P. Howe), 7 bottom, 27 top, 34, 43, 76, 77 bottom, 93, 100, 120 (Tony Morrison)

Superstock, Inc.: 19 (age fotostock), 16, 131 bottom (Carlos Adolfo Sastoque N.)

The Art Archive/Picture Desk: 54 (Dagli Orti/Museo 20 de Julio de 1810 Bogota), 44 (Dagli Orti/Museo del Oro Bogota), 47 (Dagli Orti/Museo Nacional Bogota)

The Image Works: 75 (Timothy Ross), 107 (Topham)

Victor Englebert: 7 top, 24

Maps by XNR Productions, Inc.